FISH TRADITIONS: MEMBER RECIPES

FISH TRADITIONS: MEMBER RECIPES

North American Fishing Club
Minnetonka, Minnesota

Acknowledgements

Fish Traditions: Member Recipes

We would like to thank NAFC members
for sending their favorite fish recipes as the
foundation for *Fish Traditions: Member Recipes.*

Tom Carpenter
Creative Director

Michele Teigen
Senior Book Development Coordinator

Zins Design Studio
Book Design and Production

Mowers Photography
Photography

Mary Lane
Food Stylist

11 12 13 14 15 16 / 13 12 11 10 09 08
ISBN 10: 1-58159-049-0
ISBN 13: 978-1-58159-049-4
© 1999 North American Fishing Club

North American Fishing Club
12301 Whitewater Drive
Minnetonka, MN 55343
www.fishingclub.com

Special Note

The North American Fishing club proudly presents this special cookbook edition which includes the personal favorites of your fellow Members. Each recipe has been screened by a cooking professional and edited for clarity. However, we are not able to kitchen-test these recipes and cannot guarantee their outcome, or your safety in their preparation or consumption. Please be advised that any recipes which require the use of dangerous equipment (such as pressure cookers), or potentially unsafe preparation procedures (such as canning and pickling) should be used with caution and safe, healthy practices.

TABLE OF CONTENTS

INTRODUCTION

Use these great recipes—shared by North American Fishing Club members— to start some new fish-cooking traditions of your own!

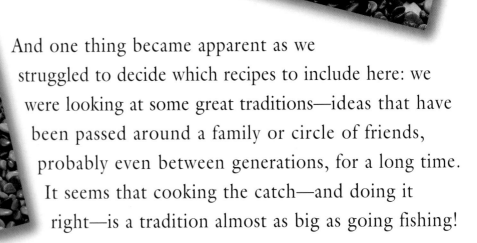

Imagine our delight upon seeing the recipes members submitted to help us create *Fish Traditions: Member Recipes*. Here were hundreds of wonderful dishes, each truly celebrating the fish at hand and using it in a unique, special and delicious way.

And one thing became apparent as we struggled to decide which recipes to include here: we were looking at some great traditions—ideas that have been passed around a family or circle of friends, probably even between generations, for a long time. It seems that cooking the catch—and doing it right—is a tradition almost as big as going fishing!

So welcome to these *Fish Traditions.* It has been your Club's privilege to receive all these great recipes and pull them together into this beautiful, photo-filled volume. Now it's your privilege to have these recipes for your own kitchen—be it at home, cottage, cabin or campfire. Maybe you'll create some great new traditions of your own—more ways to celebrate the catches you make, when you decide to keep some fish "for the pan."

So get out fishing more, then create some fish-cooking traditions as well; the recipe ideas you need are right here.

SPECIAL THANKS TO OUR AUTHORS

This book has many authors—every member who sent in a recipe, whether it appears in this book or has been saved for some future use. To all these contributors we extend a heartfelt thanks, for sharing their fish-cooking traditions: taking the time to write down these recipe jewels and share them with others who care about fishing and the incredible natural resources of clean water and healthy, wholesome fish.

General Notes on Cleaning, Handling and Filleting Fish

Anyone who has eaten his or her own catch knows that fish are best when cooked and eaten as fresh as possible, right off the hook.

Fresh Fish

For fish to be eaten soon after they are caught, de-gill and gut the fish. After thumbing out the kidneys and washing out the cavity, thoroughly dry it. Place the fish on ice or in a creel lined with dampened ferns.

If the fish are larger—salmon, steelhead or trophy-sized trout—bleed them by sticking them just behind the gill, then cover and tie them (air free) in a plastic tube. The tube should be cut off a roll with a length to accommodate the fish plus two knots. Lay the fish in the stream to keep cool.

If you are driving home with the fish and preparing the fish the next day, do not gut and gill the fish until you get home. Put the fish on ice. Pour or drain off the water as it accumulates, as water is a carrier of the bacteria that spoil flesh.

Filleting Fish

In filleting fish, try to start the process by using a fillet knife that is as flexible as possible and has a narrow blade curving to a sharp point. It should also be razor sharp.

Lay the fish on a board; cut down to the spine and around the sides. Do not cut the spine in two. Cut into fish behind the transverse cut and slice toward the tail, cutting down to, but not through, the ribcage. When you have sliced down two-thirds of the length of the fish (where it begins to taper), push the point clear through, keeping the flat of the blade close along the backbone. Holding the fish with the left hand, continue to cut close against the backbone all the way to the tail. Now lay the fillet open and finish cutting the flesh away from the ribcage. Slice it loose along the belly line, turn the fish over, and duplicate process on the other side.

To remove skin, place the fillet on the board, skin side down, and take hold of the tip of the fillet with the left hand. Cut in between skin and flesh, then change your grip with the left hand. Hold tight onto the skin tip while you slice forward, pressing the flat of the knife blade down as you slice forward.

Freezing Fish

Fish kept on ice will remain reasonably flavorful for two days. Do not keep fish longer than four to eight hours in the refrigerator before freezing. All fish deteriorates in flavor after frozen, but you can reduce this deterioration markedly by freezing the fish in a block of ice or with a thin layer of ice over its surface.

Cookbook Abbreviations

tsp. = teaspoon(s)
T. = tablespoon(s)
oz. = ounce(s)
pkg. = package(s)
qt. = quart
lb. = pound

Measurement Conversions

1 pinch = less than ⅛ tsp.
1 T. = 3 tsp.
2 T. = 1 oz.
4 T. = ¼ cup
5 T. + 1 tsp. = ⅓ cup
8 T. = ½ cup
16 T. = 1 cup

1 cup = 8 oz.
1 pint = 16 oz.
1 quart = 32 oz.
1 gallon = 128 oz.

1 cup = ½ pint
2 cups = 1 pint
4 cups = 1 quart
2 pints = 1 quart
4 pints = ½ gallon
8 pints = 1 gallon
4 quarts = 1 gallon
8 gallons = 1 bushel

BASS

Even in these days of

catch-and-release, it's okay to keep

a few bass to eat now and then

if the resource allows for it.

And bass—largemouths, smallmouths

as well as stripers—is good: white,

firm, with a taste all its own.

Try some of these traditional favorites

next time you have a bass or two to cook.

Grilled Bass

Bass fillets, skin and scales on

Butter

1 onion, chopped

Salt

Pepper

Lemon juice

Favorite spices

Prepare grill. Cook fillets scale-side down. Apply butter, onion, salt, pepper, lemon juice and any other desired spices to meat side of fish. Cook until fish flakes easily with a fork. Do not turn fish. Peel skin and scales off fish. Enjoy.

Lee Phillips
Zebulon, NC

Oriental Bass Steaks

2 lbs. bass steaks

$1/4$ cup orange juice

$1/4$ cup soy sauce

2 T. ketchup

2 T. oil

2 T. chopped parsley

1 T. lemon juice

1 clove garlic, finely chopped

$1/2$ tsp. oregano

$1/2$ tsp. pepper

Cut steaks into serving-size portions. Place in single layer in baking dish. Combine remaining ingredients. Pour sauce over fish. Let stand for 30 minutes; turning once. Remove fish; reserve sauce for basting. Place fish in well-oiled, hinged wire grill. Cook 4 inches from moderately hot coals for 8 minutes. Baste with sauce. Turn; cook for 7-10 minutes or until fish flakes easily with a fork.

Jim Gallant
Yarmouthport, ME

Spicy Smoked White Bass

1 qt. water

¹/₄ cup salt

White bass fillets, skin on

Barbecue sauce

Cayenne pepper

1 T. tarragon

Dissolve salt in water, place fillets in brine; soak overnight. Rinse fillets, place on racks skin-side down. Air dry 30 minutes. Brush with barbecue sauce; lightly sprinkle with cayenne pepper. Add tarragon to smoker water pan. Smoke 3 hours with charcoal pan half full, water pan two-thirds full.

Cam Powers
Mason City, IA

Joyce's Key Lime Striper

2 lbs. striper fillets

1 tsp. salt

Dash of black pepper

¹/₄ cup lime juice

3 T. butter, melted

Paprika

Lime wedges

Skin fillets, remove and discard red meat. Cut remaining fish into serving-size portions. Place fillets in single layer in baking dish. Sprinkle with salt and pepper. Pour lime juice over fish; let stand 30 minutes, turning once. Remove fish, reserve juice. Place fish on well-oiled broiler pan. Combine butter with juice; brush fish with mixture. Sprinkle with paprika. Broil 4 inches from heat source 8-10 minutes or until fish flakes easily with fork. Serve with lime wedges.

Rick Beaudry
Pagosa Springs, CO

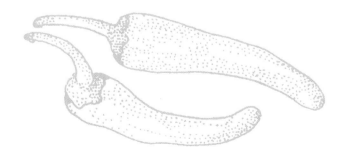

Cornflake Bass

Cornflake Bass

1 cup mayonnaise

1 tsp. lemon juice

Salt

Pepper

Bass fillets

5 cups crushed cornflakes

Combine mayonnaise, lemon juice, salt and pepper. Dip fillets in mixture and then in bowl of crushed cornflakes. Bake at 350 degrees for 10-15 minutes.

Lee Phillips
Zebulon, NC

Quick Microwave Bass

$^1/_2$ cup finely chopped onion

2 T. butter

1 can cream of celery soup

$^1/_4$ cup dry white wine

1 cup grated Swiss cheese

1 T. lemon juice

2 tsp. chopped parsley

1 lb. bass fillets

2 T. dried bread crumbs

Paprika

Combine onion and butter in 2 quart glass baking dish. Microwave on high for 3 minutes. Stir in soup, wine, cheese, lemon juice and parsley. Arrange fillets in sauce, making sure to coat both sides. Sprinkle with bread crumbs and paprika. Microwave on high for 7 minutes. Let stand for 5 minutes before serving.

Rick Beaudry
Pagosa Springs, CO

Jaime's Bass Fillets

4 striped bass fillets

Juice of $^{1}/_{2}$ lemon

Salt

1 T. butter, melted

1 T. flour

Paprika

1 can cream of mushroom soup

1 T. sweet cream

1 T. grated Parmesan cheese

Parsley

Wipe fillets with damp cloth; sprinkle with drops of lemon juice and salt. Melt butter in saucepan; blend in flour and paprika. Cook 4 minutes, stirring constantly. Add mushroom soup. Remove from fire; stir until completely mixed. Arrange fillets in shallow baking dish; pour sweet cream over. Pour hot mushroom sauce over fillets; sift grated Parmesan cheese over top. Bake at 350 degrees for 15 minutes. Garnish with parsley.

Jim Gallant
Yarmouthport, MA

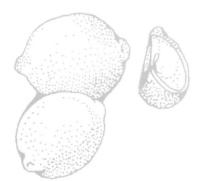

Poached Bass

Fish:

Salt

Pepper

6 bass fillets

Water

2 stalks celery, sliced

2 sprigs parsley

1 onion, sliced

1 whole clove

Egg and Parsley Sauce:

2 cups medium white sauce

1 egg, beaten

$^{1}/_{2}$ tsp. dry mustard

$^{1}/_{2}$ tsp. Worcestershire sauce

Salt

Pepper

2 T. chopped parsley

Salt and pepper fillets. Place fillets in large skillet; cover with water. Add celery, parsley, onion and clove. Poach for 30 minutes. Serve with egg and parsley sauce.

To prepare sauce, add egg to white sauce; combine. Add remaining ingredients except parsley. Heat; stirring until thick and smooth. Add chopped parsley. Serve individual slices of fish covered with warmed sauce. Top with hard-boiled egg slice. Garnish with sprig of parsley. Place wedge of lime or lemon on side.

Mr. Roy Timberlake
Buffalo, NY

Oven-Broiled Largemouth Bass

6 strips bacon

1 onion, chopped

1 cup chopped apple

2 lemons, thinly sliced

1 green pepper, chopped

4 lbs. bass, filleted

1 T. salt

1 tsp. pepper

1 cup butter

1 cup Worcestershire sauce

2 T. soy sauce

1 tsp. garlic powder

1 tsp. celery salt

Place 3 strips bacon in bottom of shallow baking pan. In a separate bowl, mix onion, apple, lemon and green pepper. Layer a third of mixture on bacon strips. Sprinkle both sides of fish with salt and pepper. Place fish on vegetable mixture. Place a third mixture into fish cavity and remaining third on top of fish. Place 3 strips bacon on top of vegetable mixture. Melt butter in saucepan. Add Worcestershire and soy sauce. Add remaining ingredients; boil. Pour sauce over fish. Bake at 375 degrees, basting until meat separates from bones.

Shawn Jennings
Evans, CO

Fish Kabobs

1 lb. bacon

2-3 bass fillets

1 cup ketchup

$1/3$ cup brown sugar

1 T. lemon juice

Cut bacon in half. Fry until soft. Drain; reserve bacon. Cut fish into 2-inch strips. Combine ketchup, brown sugar and lemon juice in bowl. Add fish to bowl; mix well. Take fish out of bowl; place on cookie sheet. Wrap each piece of fish with bacon; secure with toothpick. Bake at 350 degrees for 10 minutes or until done.

James Wicks
Kenosha, WI

Grilled Bass in Foil

Water

2 bass fillets

Juice of 2 lemons

2 tsp. black pepper

3 green onions, finely chopped

Tear off sheet of aluminum foil large enough to fold up and loosely cover fish. Fold up all sides of foil to create 6-inch sides. Cover bottom of foil "dish" with 1/4-inch of water. Place fillets in water; add lemon juice. Sprinkle pepper evenly over fillets. Place green onions in water around fillets. Fold sides over fillets to cover; pinch together to seal. Place on grill; cook for 15-25 minutes or until fish flakes.

Tim Vann
La Porte, IN

Long Island Surf Steaks

Marinade:

1/4 cup unsweetened iced tea mix

1 3/4 cups ginger ale

Juice of 2 fresh lemons

1/2 T. black pepper

1/3 cup light soy sauce

1 T. peeled, minced, gingerroot

1 handful minced fresh mint leaves, stems discarded

Fish:

6-8 striped bass steaks

Wasabi (green horseradish sauce)

Fresh parsley

Combine all marinade ingredients. Pour into zip top storage bags. Add steaks. Place in refrigerator for 4 to 6 hours, turning at least once. Place steaks on aluminum foil sprayed with nonstick cooking spray. Spread thin layer of wasabi on top of each steak. Bake at 400 degrees for 25 minutes. Broil steaks for a few minutes to lightly brown tops. Garnish with parsley.

Richard Zablauskas
Bronx, NY

Long Island Surf Steaks

CATFISH

Catfish may lack beauty

in the water, but they make up for it

on the dinner plate. Same with

bullheads—they run on the small side,

they're not pretty—but like catfish,

a mess cooks up wonderfully

when you use recipe traditions

like the ones you'll find here.

Rio Grande Blackened Catfish

1/2 tsp. red pepper

1 tsp. garlic salt

1 tsp. thyme

1/2 tsp. black pepper

1/2 lb. butter

Juice of 1 lemon

Catfish fillets, 1/2 inch thick, 4-5 inches long

Fresh cilantro

Combine seasonings; mix well. Melt butter in skillet; set aside. Heat separate skillet as hot as possible. Stir lemon juice into melted butter skillet. Sprinkle fillets with seasoning mixture. Dip fillets in butter and drop in hot skillet. Cook 1-2 minutes, turn. There should be black crust on edge. If not, wait longer while the other side cooks. Serve with rice pilaf and tossed salad. Garnish with fresh cilantro.

Andy Ligon
El Paso, TX

Fried Bullhead

Bullheads, cleaned

Milk

3/4 cup flour

1/2 cup cornmeal

2 tsp. paprika

1/2 tsp. ground black pepper

1 tsp. seasoned salt

Oil

Lemon or lime wedges

Clean bullheads, cover fillets with milk; refrigerate for 3 hours. Mix dry ingredients in plastic bag. Drain and dry fillets. Place fillets in bag; shake to coat fish evenly. Heat oil in skillet. Cook fillets 2-3 minutes per side until golden brown. Serve with lemon or lime wedges and tartar sauce.

Tom Huntowski
Minong, WI

Crispy Oven-Fried Catfish

1 egg white

¹/₂ cup freshly squeezed lime juice

¹/₂ cup flour

¹/₂ cup white cornmeal

1 tsp. lemon pepper

¹/₂ tsp. cayenne pepper

¹/₄ tsp. black pepper

1 T. coarsely chopped fresh dillweed

1¹/₂ tsp. dried basil

¹/₂ tsp. garlic powder

2 catfish fillets, halved

Lemon wedges

Dill sprig

Coat baking sheet with nonstick spray. In bowl, whisk together egg white and lime juice. Place flour in shallow dish. In separate bowl, combine cornmeal, peppers, dill, basil and garlic powder. Dip each fillet in flour, shake off excess. Then dip in egg white mixture, allowing excess to drip off. Roll each piece in cornmeal mixture. Place fillets on baking sheet; coat lightly with nonstick cooking spray. Bake 5 minutes, turn, bake another 5 minutes or until brown and crisp. Serve with lemon wedge and dill sprig garnish.

Norma A. Blank
Shawano, WI

Pan-Fried Cajun Catfish

1¹/₃ lbs. catfish fillets

Creole seasoning

1 T. olive oil

Sprinkle both sides of fillets generously with Creole seasoning. Heat oil to medium in skillet. Cook fillets in oil, 3 minutes on each side or until just cooked throughout.

Justin Jankuv
McDonough, NY

Grilled Catfish Mexicana

Grilled Catfish Mexicana

Combine milk and cumin in large, plastic, zip top food-storage bag. Add fillets, turning to coat. Seal bag. Chill 1 hour. In 8-inch skillet, heat oil over medium heat. Reduce heat to low. Stir in onion, chopped pepper, cilantro, salt and pepper. Simmer, uncovered for 1-2 minutes, or until chopped pepper is tender-crisp. Set aside. Drain milk mixture from fillets; discard. Cut four 14 x 12-inch sheets of heavy-duty aluminum foil. Place 1 fillet on each sheet of foil. Top each fillet with one-fourth vegetable mixture and 1 teaspoon taco sauce. Fold long sides of foil together in locked folds. Fold and crimp short ends; seal tightly. Place foil packs on grill grate. Grill, covered for 11-17 minutes, or until fish is firm and opaque. Garnish with lemon and lime wedges.

William Pugh
Cleveland, OH

¹/₂ cup milk

¹/₂ tsp. ground cumin

1¹/₂ lbs. catfish fillets, skin removed

2 T. olive oil

1 medium onion, finely chopped

¹/₂ cup chopped green, yellow or red pepper

¹/₄ cup fresh snipped cilantro leaves

¹/₄ tsp. salt

¹/₄ tsp. freshly ground pepper

4 tsp. taco sauce or salsa (optional)

Lemon wedges

Lime wedges

Broiled Lemon Pepper Catfish

4 catfish fillets

Lemon pepper seasoning

¹/₄ cup lemon juice

¹/₄ cup Worcestershire sauce

¹/₄ cup Italian dressing

Dust fillets with lemon pepper. Combine lemon juice, Worcestershire and Italian dressing. Baste fillets with sauce. Broil fillets on high until golden brown.

The Brewers
Hillsboro, OH

Skillet Fried
Catfish Nuggets

1 cup milk

1 egg

1 sleeve saltine crackers, finely crushed

1 tsp. seasoned salt

*2 lbs. catfish fillets, cut into
1-inch strips*

Oil

Catfish Bites

^{3}/4 cup bread crumbs

1 tsp. paprika

^{1}/4 tsp. salt

*1^1/3 lbs. catfish fillets, cut into
bite-size pieces*

^{1}/2 cup milk

Mix milk and egg. Combine crackers and seasoned salt. Dip fillets in milk mixture, then roll in cracker mixture. Heat oil to medium heat in skillet. Fry fillets for 3 minutes on each side.

Lee Brown
Farris, OK

Combine bread crumbs, paprika and salt. Dip fish in milk, roll in crumb mixture. Coat baking sheet lightly with nonstick cooking spray. Place fillets on sheet. Bake at 500 degrees for 8 minutes, until crispy and browned. Serve with tartar sauce.

Justin G. Jankuv
McDonough, NY

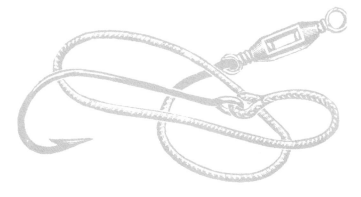

Catfish Nuggets

1 egg, beaten

1 T. Worcestershire sauce

1 cup cornmeal

Catfish fillets

$^1/_2$ cup oil

2 T. butter

4 cloves garlic

White pepper

Lemon wedges

Combine egg and Worcestershire sauce. Place cornmeal in large, plastic zip top bag. Dip catfish in egg mixture, then place in cornmeal; shake to coat. Place catfish on wax-paper. Heat oil and butter in skillet. Add garlic, stir to blend. Add catfish; cook until fish flakes easily with a fork. Season with white pepper. Serve with lemon wedges.

Mike and Ginger Roy
Via e-mail

Catfish Coating

1 cup crushed cornflakes

$^1/_4$ cup Parmesan cheese

1 T. parsley

$^1/_2$ tsp. salt

$^1/_4$ tsp. oregano

$^1/_2$ tsp. basil

$^1/_4$ tsp. pepper

$^1/_2$ tsp. celery salt

$^1/_2$ tsp. onion salt

$^1/_4$ tsp. paprika

Catfish fillets

1 box lard

Combine all ingredients, except fish and lard, in large mixing bowl. Dip fillets in mixture. Heat lard in skillet. Place coated fillets in skillet. Cook until golden brown.

James Tarlton
Camp Verde, AZ

Catfish and Scallops with Mushrooms

1 cup cornmeal

Salt

Pepper

1 cup milk

1 egg

2-4 catfish fillets

$1/4$ cup oil

Scallops

Mushrooms

$1/2$ tsp. basil

Beer

$1/2$ cup chicken broth

Combine cornmeal, salt and pepper. Mix milk and egg. Place fillets in milk mixture, then roll in cornmeal mixture. Heat oil in skillet. Cook each fillet 2-5 minutes per side. Brown scallops and mushrooms with basil. Add beer and chicken broth. Cook until mushrooms are done and liquid is evaporated.

Julio Prieto
Riverton, UT

Fried Catfish

2 lbs. thin catfish fillets

2 tsp. lemon juice

1 egg, beaten

1 tsp. salt

1 tsp. milk

Dash of pepper

1 cup yellow cornmeal

Cooking oil

Cut fish into serving fillets. Sprinkle with lemon juice; let stand 15 minutes. Combine egg, salt, milk and pepper. Dip fish in egg mix; roll in cornmeal. Fry in oil until fish is golden brown. Serve with hush puppies, tartar sauce or hot sauce and tomato ketchup.

Isaac Turman
Chicago, IL

Catfish and Scallops
with Mushrooms

Catfish Spicy Coating

2 cups Bisquick

1 tsp. garlic powder

1 T. paprika

1 T. chili powder

$1/2$ tsp. cayenne pepper

Salt

Pepper

2 eggs

1 T. water

Oil

Catfish fillets

Combine all dry ingredients. In a separate bowl, combine all wet ingredients. Dredge fillets in dry ingredients, then in wet ingredients, then back to dry ingredients. Heat oil in skillet. Fry fish in oil until golden brown.

Gary R. Coon Sr.
Newark, DE

Catfish and Fries

$1/4$ tsp. salt

$1/4$ tsp. black pepper

$1/8$ tsp. cayenne pepper

$1/4$ tsp. thyme leaves

$3/4$ cup flour

$1^{1}/2$-2 lbs. catfish, cut into bite-size pieces

Oil

1-2 lbs. potatoes, cut into $2^{1}/2$-inch sticks

$1/4$ tsp. salt

2 tsp. lemon juice

2 T. butter, melted

Tomatoes

Onions

Soy sauce

Combine salt, black pepper, cayenne pepper, thyme and flour in a bag. Shake catfish fillets in bag. Heat oil in skillet. Fry fish until golden brown, 5-7 minutes. Fry potatoes in hot oil in nonstick skillet. Mix potatoes and fish on large platter. Sprinkle with salt, lemon juice and melted butter. Serve with sliced tomatoes and sliced onions sprinkled with soy sauce.

Paul H. Wells
Sierra Vista, AZ

Quick Cajun Catfish

1/4 cup buttermilk

2 tsp. Dijon mustard

1/2 cup cornmeal

1 tsp. salt

1 tsp. paprika

1 tsp. onion powder

1/2 tsp. garlic powder

1/2 tsp. dried thyme leaves

1/2 tsp. ground red pepper

1/2 tsp. freshly ground black pepper

4 catfish fillets

4 lemon wedges

Lightly oil wire rack large enough to hold fillets in single layer. Place rack on baking sheet; set aside. In medium bowl, whisk together buttermilk and mustard until smooth. In shallow dish, combine cornmeal, salt, paprika, onion powder, garlic powder, thyme, ground red pepper and black pepper. Dip each fillet in buttermilk mixture, turning to coat. Transfer fillets to cornmeal mixture, turning to coat. Place fillets on prepared wire rack. Broil 4 inches from heat, until fish is opaque in center, about 3 minutes per side. Serve hot with lemon wedges.

Leo G. J. Seffelaar
Broadview, Saskatchewan, Canada

Tangy Orange Catfish

Marinade:

1/4 cup orange juice

2 T. vegetable oil

2 T. soy sauce

1 T. lemon juice

1 tsp. minced garlic

1/8 tsp. pepper

Fish:

4 catfish fillets

Mix marinade ingredients in large, plastic, zip top bag. Place fish fillets in bag. Seal and refrigerate for 3 hours, turning bag several times. Line broiler pan with foil. Coat broiler pan rack with nonstick spray, set rack in pan. Arrange fillets in single layer. Broil 4 inches from heat for 10 minutes, turning fish once.

Norma Blank
Shawano, WI

31

Bullhead Marinated
in Barbecue Sauce

Bullhead Marinated in Barbecue Sauce

In small skillet, cook onions in olive oil over medium heat until onions are tender, about 3 minutes. Stir in brown sugar, ketchup, vinegar, Worcestershire sauce, dry mustard, salt, pepper and oregano. Cook, stirring occasionally, until mixture is bubbly. Reduce heat, simmer; stir occasionally for 10 minutes. Place bullheads in medium bowl. Pour marinade over fish. Cover, refrigerate for 30 minutes, turning fish at least once. Grease broiler pan. Remove fish from marinade with slotted spoon. Place on broiler pan. Broil at 550 degrees for 8 minutes. Baste with marinade; turn once. Broil 8 more minutes or until fish flakes easily.

Roland J. Cote III
Waterville, ME

3 T. chopped onions

1 T. olive oil

1/4 cup packed brown sugar

1/4 cup ketchup

1/4 cup cider vinegar

2 T. Worcestershire sauce

1/2 tsp. dry mustard

1/4 tsp. salt

1/4 tsp. black pepper

1/8 tsp. dried oregano leaves

1 1/2-2 lbs. bullheads, heads and skin removed

Stovetop Catfish

1 can beer

2 cups crushed Stove Top stuffing

Oil

2 (1-lb.) catfish fillets

Leave beer open in refrigerator overnight. Combine stuffing and beer to make batter. Pour oil into skillet. Heat to medium. Dip catfish in batter; coat well. Fry fish in oil until fish is opaque and flakes easily with a fork.

Mae Renner
Via e-mail

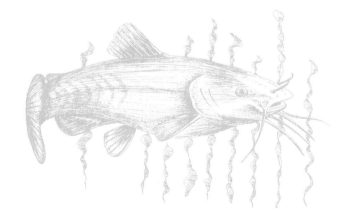

PANFISH

Abundant, willing to bite, good fighters

for their size, firm and sweet meat

that can't be beat ... panfish were made

for catching and for eating. Whether it's bluegill

or bream, shellcrackers, crappie, yellow perch

or something else, cooking panfish is a

taste-filled tradition across North America.

Most of these recipes will work with species

other than the one specified; it's the ideas

that count here!

Bread and Butter Pickles with Pickled Fish

6 large onions

1 gallon sliced cucumbers

$^1/_2$ cup salt

Water

4 cups sugar

$^1/_2$ T. turmeric

$^1/_2$ tsp. mustard seed

$1^1/_4$ qts. vinegar

Raw panfish pieces

Combine onion, cucumbers, salt and enough water to cover all. Weight down ingredients and let stand 3 hours. Drain; add sugar, turmeric, mustard seed and vinegar. Place over slow fire; boil. Cut raw fish into small pieces. Add fish to bread and butter pickles. Place in canning jars and seal.

Ron and Becky Zirkel
Medora, IN

Panfish Casserole

1 lb. panfish fillets, skinned

9-inch pie crust shell

$^1/_4$ cup sliced black olives

$^1/_2$ cup chopped red pepper

$^1/_2$ cup chopped fresh mushrooms

2 scallions, chopped

4 eggs

$^1/_4$ cup half and half cream

$^3/_4$ cup ricotta cheese

$^1/_2$ tsp. thyme leaves

$^1/_4$ tsp. paprika

Salt

Pepper

Cut fillets into pieces $1^1/_2$ inches long and 1 inch wide. Layer olives and vegetables in bottom of pie shell. Lay fish evenly over vegetable mixture. In separate bowl, combine remaining ingredients. Mix well; pour over fish. Place on baking sheet with sides. Fill sheet with $^1/_4$-inch water. Bake at 350 degrees for 35-40 minutes. Let cool before serving.

Roger McKeon
Penfield, NY

Lemon Fish

Panfish fillets

2 T. lemon juice

Pepper

Place fillets in skillet. Add lemon juice; sprinkle with pepper. Sauté for 15-20 minutes over medium-low heat.

Jeff Petersik
Milwaukee, WI

Zesty Bluegill Burgers

16 bluegills, filleted, boiled, chopped

1 cup bread crumbs

$^1/_4$ cup finely chopped onions

$^1/_4$ cup mayonnaise

2 T. prepared horseradish

$^1/_8$ tsp. pepper

Butter

Combine all ingredients except butter; mix well. Shape into patties. Fry in butter until browned. Serve on Kaiser rolls with choice of topping.

William Muntz
Streator, IL

Beer Batter Panfish

2 cups oil

$1^1/_2$ cups buttermilk pancake mix

1 egg

1 tsp. salt

$1^1/_2$ tsp. white pepper

$^1/_2$ tsp. thyme

$1^1/_2$ cups beer

2 lbs. panfish fillets

Pour oil into skillet; heat to 375 degrees. Mix remaining ingredients, except fillets; set aside. Season fillets with salt and pepper. Slice fillets into finger-size pieces. Dip fillets into batter; allow excess to drip off. Place pieces in skillet one at a time; fry until golden brown. Drain on paper towels. Serve with lemon wedge.

Robert Buschelman
Cincinnati, OH

Panfish Chowder

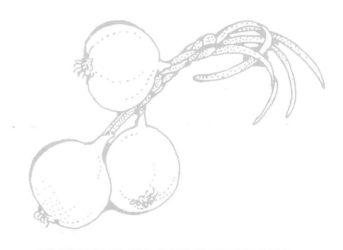

Panfish Chowder

Prepare sachet herb bag by placing bay leaf, thyme, peppercorns and dried dill in cheesecloth. Tie securely with twine so herbs don't filter into stock. In large skillet, simmer salted water. Add fish bones, lemon slices and sachet bag. Simmer for 45-60 minutes. Remove bones and lemon slices. Add fillets and poach until fish flakes with fork, but remains firm.

Remove fish to plate and discard sachet bag. Bring remaining stock to a full boil. Add diced potatoes; cook until tender. Add water if necessary to keep potatoes covered. While potatoes are cooking, brown bacon in soup pot. Add onions and sauté until transparent. Add 4-5 tablespoons flour if you desire thicker chowder; cook 10 more minutes. Add stock and cooked potatoes to onion mixture in soup pot; combine thoroughly. Add cooked fish and cream; combine. Boil, then reduce heat. Add butter. When butter is melted, season to taste with salt and pepper.

Roger McKeon
Penfield, NY

1 bay leaf

1 tsp. thyme leaves

6-8 black peppercorns

1 tsp. dried dill

$1\frac{1}{2}$ qts. water

$1\frac{1}{2}$ lbs. fish fillets, skinned
(save bones, discard skin and head)

2 lemon slices

$1\frac{1}{2}$ lbs. potatoes, peeled, diced

3 strips bacon, diced

2 medium onions, diced

$2\frac{1}{2}$ cups light cream

2 T. butter

Salt

White pepper

Emergency Summertime Panfish BBQ

In a large bowl, add butter, herbs and spices; mix well. Add all fillets and vegetables to mixture. Stir mixture for several minutes; until panfish are well coated. Cut lemons in half, remove seeds and squeeze juice into bowl. Stir one more minute. Tear off a two-foot sheet of aluminum foil. Double foil over; fold ends and sides up to form "bowl." Pour fish mixture into middle of "bowl." Tear off another sheet of foil to cover fish; fold sides and ends together to seal with bottom foil. Place on heated barbecue over medium flame for 10 minutes. Flip package; cook for another 10 minutes. Remove, open and serve.

Shawn P. Good
Pittsford, VT

$2/3$ cup butter, melted

1 tsp. paprika

1 tsp. tarragon

1 tsp. garlic powder

$1/2$ tsp. cayenne pepper

1 tsp. crushed black peppercorns

1 tsp. sea salt

40-50 panfish fillets, boneless, skinless

2 stalks celery, diced

2 medium carrots, finely diced

2 medium red sweet onions, finely diced

1 medium green bell pepper, diced

1 medium red sweet bell pepper, diced

$1/2$ lb. mushrooms, sliced

2 fresh lemons

Crappie Delight

2 cups yellow cornmeal

2 bags barbecue potato chips, finely crumbled

2 lbs. crappie fillets

Cooking oil

1 tsp. salt

$1/2$ tsp. pepper

Place cornmeal and potato chips in bag. Wash fillets. Place in bag; shake until fillets are well-coated. Heat oil to 350 degrees. Fry fish 2-3 minutes. Salt and pepper to taste.

Jerry Dunn
Via e-mail

Pickled Crappie

2¹/₂ cups white vinegar

1 tsp. salt

40 peppercorns

6 bay leaves

20 crappie fillets

6 medium onions, peeled, sliced

Boil vinegar, salt, peppercorns and bay leaves in saucepan; cool. Cut crappie fillets into chunks; put into 2 quart jars. Add onion rings to each jar. Pour cooled mixture into each jar; tighten lids. Let stand for 24 hours. Store in refrigerator.

Norma Blank
Shawano, WI

Red Sauce Poached Perch

1 T. minced garlic

2 T. olive oil

1 large can chopped tomatoes

¹/₂ tsp. dried basil

¹/₂ tsp. fennel seeds

¹/₂ tsp. salt

¹/₂ tsp. pepper

1 lb. perch fillets

Place all ingredients, except perch, in saucepan. Simmer for 10-15 minutes. Rinse fillets; place in glass baking dish. Pour sauce over fish. Poach at 350 degrees until flaky. Serve with thick garlic bread slices.

Robert J. Duquette
Fall River, MA

Parmesan Fish

8 panfish fillets

Butter

Salt

Pepper

Garlic salt

Italian seasoning

1 can tomato soup

Parmesan cheese

Place fillets in buttered skillet. Season with salt, pepper, garlic salt and Italian seasoning. Sear fillets; place in baking dish; cover with tomato soup. Bake at 350 degrees for 30 minutes. Place Parmesan cheese over each fillet; cook until cheese is melted. Place cooked soup on plate; lay fillet on top; serve.

David Miller
Via e-mail

Bayou Bank Spicy Fried Fish

Panfish fillets

12-oz. bottle hot sauce

Garlic powder

Black pepper

$^1/_2$ lb. yellow cornmeal

$^1/_4$ cup flour

Oil

Place fillets in large bowl. Pour hot sauce in bowl; marinate 1 hour. Pour garlic powder, pepper, cornmeal and flour in bag. Remove fillets from marinade; drop in bag. Shake well coating fillets. Fry in oil until golden brown.

Pete Reno
West Monroe, LA

Parmesan Fish

Louisiana Panfish

3 cups buttermilk

4-oz. Louisiana Hot Sauce

30 panfish fillets

$^3/_4$ tsp. salt

$^3/_4$ tsp. pepper

$1^1/_2$ T. Creole seasoning

3 cups yellow cornmeal

Mix buttermilk and hot sauce. Marinate fillets in mixture for 2 hours. Salt and pepper fillets. Mix Creole seasoning and cornmeal together in bag. Put several fillets in bag and shake. Deep fry fillets in hot oil until golden brown.

Norma A. Blank
Shawano, WI

Bluegill Parmesan

$^1/_4$ cup margarine, melted

$^1/_2$ cup bread crumbs

$^1/_3$ cup grated Parmesan cheese

2 T. minced fresh parsley

1 tsp. salt

$^1/_2$ tsp. paprika

$^1/_4$ tsp. pepper

$^1/_4$ tsp. oregano

$^1/_4$ tsp. basil

1 lb. bluegill fillets

Place margarine in shallow dish. In a separate dish combine bread crumbs, cheese and seasonings. Dip fillets in butter; coat with crumb mixture. Place in greased 15 x 10 x 1-inch pan. Bake at 350 degrees for 20 minutes.

William Muntz
Streator, IL

Favorite Bluegill

Bluegill fillets

Tartar sauce

Cocktail sauce

Boil fillets for 30-45 seconds; until just firm. Rinse well several times. Chill in refrigerator for several hours. Serve with tartar and cocktail sauce.

Jeannine D. Hinnkle
Sparta, WI

Perky Perch Chow-da

1 lb. perch fillets, diced

4 medium potatoes, diced

1 can cream of mushroom soup

$^{1}/_{2}$ gallon milk

Salt

Pepper

Mix all ingredients together in large saucepan. Cook 1$^{1}/_{2}$-2 hours. Simmer, do not boil. Add instant potatoes to thicken if needed.

Mark and Tori Kenney
Brunswick, ME

Bluegill Italiano

1 tsp. oregano

1 tsp. cayenne pepper

1 tsp. salt

$^{1}/_{4}$ cup olive oil

2 lbs. bluegill, pan-dressed

Mix all ingredients except bluegill. Place bluegills on aluminum foil; spoon half of mixture on bluegills. Cook on grill, bake until flaky; spoon on the rest of the sauce.

Shane Felber
Kankakee, IL

Bluegill Burgers

Bluegill Burgers

1 pint bluegills, filleted, boiled, chopped fine

$\frac{1}{2}$ cup bread crumbs

2 eggs, lightly beaten

$\frac{1}{4}$ cup finely chopped celery

$\frac{1}{4}$ cup finely chopped onions

Salt

Pepper

Combine all ingredients; shape into patties. Fry over medium heat for 3-4 minutes. Serve on hamburger buns with choice of topping.

William Muntz
Streator, IL

Deep-Fried Crappie

Crappie fillets

Buttermilk

Cracker crumbs or cornmeal

Oil

Soak fillets in buttermilk 1 hour. Drain; roll in cracker crumbs. Deep fry until golden brown.

William Baker
Deltona, FL

Beer-Fried Fish

6 small perch

1 beer

1 cup flour

$\frac{1}{2}$ cup cornmeal

1 tsp. salt

$\frac{1}{2}$ tsp. pepper

4 cups hot oil

Put fish in bowl. Pour in beer; cover fish well. Marinate for 2 hours in refrigerator. Mix flour, cornmeal, salt and pepper. Remove fish from beer; reserve beer. Coat fish in flour mixture. Shake off extra. Dip fish in reserved beer; coat in flour mixture again. Deep fry until golden brown.

James and Cindy Bell
Ft. Lewis, WA

PIKE

For many people's money, a northern pike

is the best-tasting gamefish that swims.

To those who have never eaten a pike before,

alas … maybe these recipes will give you

the incentive to try one. If you already

know the pleasures of eating pike,

here are some fine ideas for enjoying

it in even more ways. Pike is firm and white,

so these recipe traditions will interchange

well with other gamefish you may have.

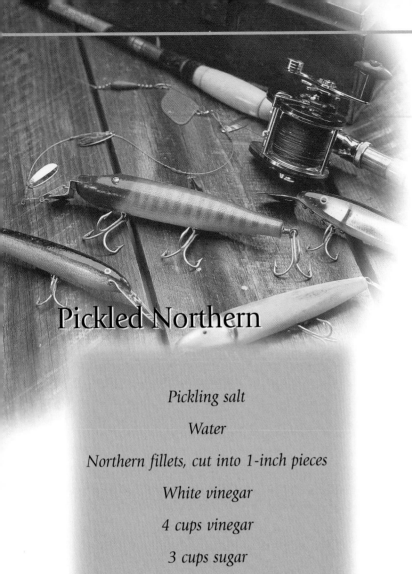

Pagosa Pickled Pike

Brine:

1¹/₂ cups table salt

1 gallon water

Fish:

6 lbs. pike fillets, cut into chunks

4 cups distilled white vinegar

8 bay leaves

2 tsp. whole cloves

2 tsp. whole black pepper

2¹/₂ cups sugar

4 tsp. mustard seed

2 tsp. whole allspice

Onions, sliced

Combine brine ingredients together. Soak pike chunks in brine for 2 days; keep refrigerated. Drain brine and soak fillets in vinegar. Refrigerate for 7-10 days; stir every couple days. When fish has finished soaking, combine all other ingredients except onions and fish in saucepan. Boil slowly for 5 minutes. Cool. Drain vinegar soaked pike chunks. Pack fish into pint jars, alternating layers of fish with onion. Pour spiced vinegar mix over fish; refrigerate 2 more days. Enjoy.

Rich Beaudry
Pagosa Springs, CO

Pickled Northern

Pickling salt

Water

Northern fillets, cut into 1-inch pieces

White vinegar

4 cups vinegar

3 cups sugar

1 cup white wine

¹/₂ box pickling spices

1 onion, sliced

Combine pickling salt and water. Soak fish in brine mixture for 48 hours. Drain well; cover with white vinegar for 24 hours. (Don't use metal container.) Boil 4 cups vinegar on stove. Remove; stir in sugar and white wine. Add pickling spices. Pack alternate layers of fish and onions into jars or plastic containers. Cover with marinade. Store in refrigerator for a couple days.

Alvin J. Dvorak
Hopkins, MN

Pike Thermidor

5 T. butter

2 lbs. pike fillets

1$\frac{1}{2}$ tsp. salt

$\frac{1}{2}$ tsp. black pepper

$\frac{3}{4}$ tsp. seasoned salt

1$\frac{1}{4}$ cups milk

3 T. flour

1 cup grated mild cheddar cheese

3 T. sherry or wine

Paprika

Melt 2 tablespoons butter in saucepan; brush over fillets. Sprinkle with salt, pepper and seasoned salt. Roll up each fillet; place seam side down in 9 x 9-inch baking dish. Pour $\frac{1}{2}$ cup milk over fillets. Bake at 350 degrees for 25 minutes or until fish flakes easily with fork. In separate saucepan, melt remaining butter. Stir in flour; gradually add remaining milk. Cook, stirring constantly until thickened. Reduce heat; stir in cheese and wine. Spoon liquid from cooked fish. Stir $\frac{1}{4}$ cup liquid into cheese sauce. (If not using wine, increase liquid by 3 tablespoons.) Pour cheese mixture over fish. Sprinkle with paprika. Broil until cheese sauce is golden, about 1 minute.

Kenneth D. Miller
Aurora, CO

Hot and Spicy Pickerel

4 lbs. fillets

2 cloves garlic

1 jar jalapeño peppers

1 large white onion, diced

1-2 cans crushed tomatoes

1 cup lemon juice

1 cup lime juice

Salt

Parsley (optional)

Combine all ingredients. Pour in jars; refrigerate for 5 days. Enjoy.

Leonard Swendsen
Honesdale, PA

Tasty Pickled Pike

Tasty Pickled Pike

Water

1 cup pickling salt

5 lbs. northern pike fillets

white vinegar

2 cups Saturn wine

3 large onions, sliced

Final Pickling Mixture:

6 cups vinegar

3 cups sugar

1 box pickling spices

Fill wide-mouth gallon jar half full of cold water. Add pickling salt; stir until dissolved. Cut fillets into ½-inch wide chunks. Place fish into brine solution until jar is full. Refrigerate for 48 hours. Drain fish; rinse. Return fish to jar; cover with vinegar. Refrigerate for 24 hours. In saucepan, combine final pickling mixture ingredients. Boil for 10 minutes; set aside to cool. When cold, add 2 cups Saturn wine. Pour vinegar off fish; remove fish from jar. Place layer of sliced onions in jar, then layer of fish. Repeat layering until jar is nearly full. Pour spice mixture over fish; refrigerate. Will be ready to eat in 4 days.

Dale Galbreath
Morris, IL

Pickled Pike

1 lb. pike fillet, cut into 1-inch cubes

Salt

½ tsp. pickling spice

1 small onion, thinly sliced

White vinegar

Coat pike cubes with salt. Spread out on plate; cover with plastic wrap. Refrigerate 24 hours. After 24 hours, place fish in glass bowl. Stir in pickling spice, onion and just enough vinegar to coat fish. Cover; refrigerate 4-5 days before eating. Fish will whiten as it cures. Salt and vinegar will soften any tiny bones that may have been missed during filleting process.

Tom Huntowski
Minong, WI

TROUT AND SALMON

A meal of trout or salmon is special,

probably because so many of these fish—

especially trout—are released to live out their

lives, breed more, and (we hope) get caught

and released again. But a fresh trout—

or a good, firm salmon from the ocean,

a Great Lake or a river—is about as

close to "eating heaven" as an earthbound

fish-lover can get. Here are some great

traditions for enjoying this treat of fish treats.

Favorite Trout

1 whole trout

Onions, sliced

Salt

Lemon pepper

Butter

Potatoes, chopped

Clean trout by cutting from tail to head. Cut off head and clean out inside of fish. Fill inside of fish with onion, salt and lemon pepper. Pan-fry fish in butter until skin is crisp. Cook potatoes by frying in same pan.

Chuck Figgins
Cedar Creek, MO

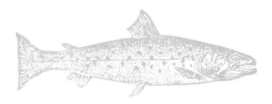

Grilled Steelhead

$3^{1}/_{2}$ lbs. steelhead, skinned, filleted

Lemon pepper

Seasoned salt

Squeeze butter

Lemon wedges

Season fish liberally with lemon pepper and seasoned salt. Rub seasonings into fillets. Arrange fillets in greased fish basket. Grill over high heat until fish is lightly browned on both sides. Before removing fish from grill, squeeze generous amount of squeeze butter on fillets. Flip basket; apply more butter. Allow butter to flame slightly; flip basket again until browned on both sides. Remove from grill. Serve with lemon wedges.

Harvey Miller
Ludington, MI

Salmon and Spinach Cannelloni with Pink Sauce

Drain tomatoes; reserve juice. Sauté onion, garlic and red pepper in oiled skillet. Pour in bowl; add salmon, spinach, herbs, ricotta cheese, egg, walnuts, tomatoes, salt and pepper. Stuff cannelloni with mixture; place in ovenproof dish. In saucepan, whisk together milk, nutmeg, flour, salt and pepper. Boil, reduce heat; stir until smooth and thick. Add cheese, stirring until it melts. Add tomato juice; boil. Pour sauce over pasta. Bake at 375 degrees for 40-45 minutes.

Leo G. J. Seffelaar
Broadview, Saskatchewan, Canada

14-oz. can of tomatoes, chopped

1 onion, minced

2 cloves garlic, minced

1 red pepper, chopped

2 tsp. oil

Salmon fillets

$^1/_2$ bag spinach, cooked, drained, chopped

$^1/_2$ tsp. dried oregano

$^1/_2$ tsp. dried basil

1 cup light ricotta cheese

1 egg, beaten

$^1/_4$ cup chopped walnuts

Salt

Pepper

12 fast-cooking cannelloni noodles

$1^1/_2$ cups milk

$^1/_2$ tsp. nutmeg

$^1/_4$ cup flour

$^1/_2$ cup grated cheddar cheese

Simple Salmon

Simple Salmon

4 salmon steaks

1 bottle Italian dressing

1 onion, diced

1 bell pepper, diced

1 tomato, diced

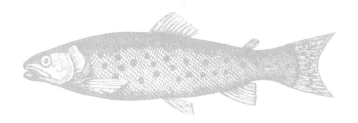

Let salmon marinate in Italian dressing for 30 minutes, turning infrequently. Separate vegetables into 4 equal portions. Wrap each salmon around 1 portion vegetables in aluminum foil. Cook on grill 3 minutes or until done.

Mark Kenney
Brunswick, ME

Pan-Fried Trout Fillets

$^1/_2$ cup flour

Paprika

Salt

Pepper

4 boned trout

2 T. vegetable oil

1 lemon, quartered

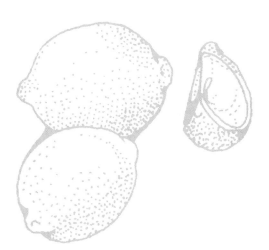

Mix flour with paprika, salt and pepper. Dip each fillet, lightly coating on both sides. Heat oil in nonstick skillet to medium. Add fillets; cook 2 minutes on each side, or until just cooked throughout. Serve with lemon wedges.

Justin Jankuv
McDonough, NY

Chardonnay Salmon Steaks

Water

Lemon juice

Salmon steaks

1 tsp. butter

$\frac{1}{2}$ tsp. salt

$\frac{1}{4}$ tsp. pepper

$\frac{1}{4}$ tsp. oregano leaves

$\frac{1}{4}$ tsp. garlic powder

$\frac{3}{4}$ cup Chardonnay wine
(dry works best)

Prepare mixture of water and lemon juice. Soak salmon steaks in mixture for 1 hour before cooking. Place salmon in oven safe dish. Place butter on salmon. Add salt, pepper, oregano and garlic powder. Submerge salmon in wine. Bake at 350 degrees for 20 minutes, or until fish flakes.

Stephen Kimball
Livonia, MI

Barbecued Salmon Fillets

1 salmon fillet

2 T. butter, melted

2 T. lemon juice

2 T. ketchup

1 T. Worcestershire sauce

2 T. minced onion

1 T. brown sugar

$\frac{1}{2}$ tsp. dry mustard

1 tsp. salt

Cut salmon fillet into 4 serving pieces. Place on greased, foil-lined baking sheet. Mix together rest of ingredients. Heat gently in saucepan; pour over salmon. Place under broiler or on well-oiled barbecue grill. Cook on one side only; allowing 10 minutes per inch thickness of fish.

Leo G. J. Seffelaar
Broadview, Saskatchewan, Canada

Smoked Trout with Horseradish Sauce

¹/₂ cup olive oil

¹/₂ cup vegetable oil

1 T. Dijon mustard

2 T. minced shallots

2 T. minced onion

1 large egg yolk

1 large egg, hard-boiled, chopped

Salt

Pepper

3 T. red or white wine vinegar

4 T. freshly grated horseradish

1 T. chopped fresh tarragon

2 T. chopped fresh parsley

4 fillets smoked trout

4 lemon wedges

Cedar Plank Salmon

¹/₄ cup olive oil

1 lemon or orange, juice and zest

1 T. chopped fresh basil

¹/₂ tsp. salt

1 tsp. freshly ground black pepper

1 salmon fillet

Combine oils in bowl. In separate bowl, combine mustard, shallots, onion, egg yolk, hard-boiled egg, salt, pepper and vinegar. Blend briskly with wire whisk. Slowly dribble oils into bowl to create emulsion. Add horseradish, tarragon and parsley. Blend well with whisk. Serve sauce around trout. Garnish each serving with lemon wedge.

Patrick Caswell
Riverside, CA

Combine all ingredients, except for salmon. Marinate salmon in mixture. Soak piece of untreated cedar plank in cold water for 2 hours (weighting it with something heavy). Bake plank in 450 degree oven for 5-10 minutes. Remove salmon from marinade. Bake on plank until cooked, allowing 10 minutes per inch thickness of fish.

Leo G. J. Seffelaar
Broadview, Saskatchewan, Canada

Warm Salmon Salad
with Soy Sesame Vinaigrette

Coat each fillet with sesame seeds; season with salt and pepper. Sauté salmon lightly in pan until cooked. Move salmon frequently so seeds don't burn. Place mixed baby greens on plate; place salmon on top. Dress with vinaigrette; garnish with sesame seeds and split strawberry.

To prepare vinaigrette, puree garlic and ginger in food processor. Add rice wine vinegar, lime juice, soy sauce and honey; mix together slowly. Add oils; continue to mix until blended. Finish by stirring in sesame seeds. Pour mixture over warm salmon salad. Serve.

Leo G. J. Seffelaar
Broadview, Saskatchewan, Canada

Fish:

4 (4 oz.) salmon fillets

4 tsp. sesame seeds

Salt

Pepper

8 cups mixed baby greens

6 tsp. soy sesame vinaigrette
(see recipe below)

6 tsp. vegetable oil

4 strawberries

Baked Salmon Fillet

¹/₂ cup mayonnaise

¹/₄ cup milk

Salmon, filleted

1 cup crushed Rice Krispies

Soy Sesame Vinaigrette:

1 clove garlic, peeled

1 T. pickled ginger

1 T. rice wine vinegar

1 T. lime juice

1 tsp. soy sauce

1 tsp. honey

2 T. vegetable oil

1 tsp. sesame oil

1 tsp. sesame seeds

Combine mayonnaise with milk. Coat fish with mayonnaise mix. Roll in Rice Krispies. Bake at 350 degrees until done.

Roger Simmons
Belfast, ME

Warm Salmon Salad

Baked Whole Trout with Sage

4 whole trout, cleaned

1 tsp. rubbed sage

3 T. margarine, melted

Salt

Pepper

Place fish in large baking pan. Mix sage and margarine; drizzle inside fish. Season cavities with salt and pepper. Bake at 425 degrees for 6-8 minutes, basting once during cooking.

Justin Jankuv
McDonough, NY

Salmon Steaks with Tomato Avocado Salsa

Fish:

4 salmon steaks

1 tsp. grated lime zest

¼ cup fresh lime juice

1 T. olive oil

1 tsp. minced fresh jalapeño pepper

Avocado Salsa:

1 tomato, diced

1 ripe avocado, peeled, diced

2 T. fresh lime juice

¼ cup minced red onion

1 tsp. minced fresh jalapeño

2 T. chopped fresh cilantro

Salt

Pepper

Marinate salmon steaks in lime zest, lime juice, olive oil and jalapeño pepper in shallow glass bowl at room temperature for 30 minutes or in refrigerator for 1 hour. Prepare barbecue grill by oiling grate. Place salmon on grill over medium heat. Cook; turn once. Baste with marinade for 4-5 minutes per side or until salmon flakes easily.

To prepare avocado salsa, combine all ingredients. Serve with salmon steaks.

Leo G. J. Seffelaar
Broadview, Saskatchewan, Canada

Ginger Mushroom Salmon

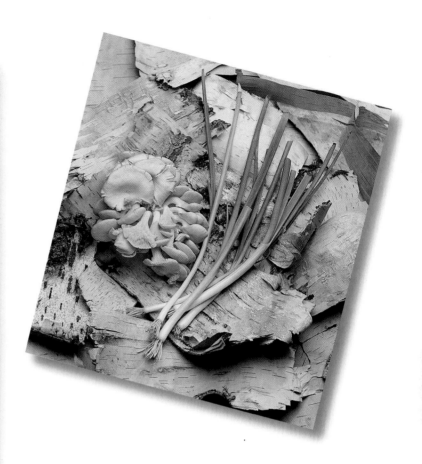

1 salmon fillet

2 T. butter

2 T. olive oil

³/₄ lb. fresh oyster mushrooms, thinly sliced

3 green onions, thinly sliced

Salt

Pepper

1 clove garlic, finely chopped

2 T. finely chopped gingerroot

2 T. fresh lemon juice

1 T. light soy sauce

Cut salmon into four serving pieces. Heat 1 tablespoon butter and 1 tablespoon olive oil in skillet; sauté mushrooms and green onions for two minutes. Stir well. Remove vegetables to warm dish; sprinkle with salt and pepper. Add remaining butter and oil to skillet; sauté salmon pieces for 4 minutes per side. Remove to another dish; keep warm. Add garlic and ginger to skillet; add extra butter and oil if necessary. Cook for 1 minute. Return mushrooms and onions to skillet. Stir in lemon juice and soy sauce; heat thoroughly. Spoon mixture over salmon pieces; serve immediately.

Leo G. J. Seffelaar
Broadview, Saskatchewan, Canada

Salmon Glazed with Honey Mustard

2 lbs. salmon fillets

3 oz. honey

4 oz. brown mustard

Rinse and dry fish; lay skin-side down in large glass baking dish. Mix honey and mustard together in bowl. Pour over salmon. Bake salmon at 350 degrees for about 15 minutes or until fish flakes easily.

Robert J. Duquette
Fall River, MA

65

Trout Amandine

Trout Amandine

Wipe fish lightly with damp paper towel. Sprinkle both sides with salt and pepper. Coat trout lightly with flour, shaking off excess. Heat 2 tablespoons butter and oil in large skillet over moderately high heat. Add trout. Cook until well-browned, about 3 minutes on each side. Turn carefully, once. In separate skillet sauté almonds in remaining 2 tablespoons butter until lightly browned; stirring occasionally. Stir in lemon juice. Sprinkle almonds lightly with salt; keep mixture warm. Arrange cooked trout in warm serving dish. Spoon almond butter over them.

Benjamin Williams
Longview, TX

4 cleaned trout

Salt

White pepper

Flour

1/4 cup butter

2 T. peanut oil

1/3 cup blanched
(sliced crosswise) almonds

2 tsp. lemon juice

67

Pan Roasted Salmon with Sweet Peppers and Garlic

1 T. olive oil

2 medium red or yellow sweet peppers

3 cloves garlic, thinly sliced

1 T. wine vinegar

2 salmon steaks

$^1/_3$ cup dry white wine

$^1/_2$ tsp. dried thyme

Pinch cayenne pepper

Salt

Pepper

Fresh parsley, chopped

Heat oil in large skillet. Sauté peppers and garlic over high heat for 1 minute, stirring constantly. Add vinegar. Cook 1 minute more; stirring. Push peppers to side of pan. Lay salmon in pan, cook 30 seconds; turn. Add wine. Sprinkle with thyme, cayenne, salt and pepper. Spoon peppers over salmon. Place lid on skillet; cook over medium heat for 6 minutes, or until fish flakes when fork-tested. Sprinkle with parsley; serve.

Leo Seffelaar
Broadview, Saskatchewan,
Canada

Trout Baked in Cream

4 whole rainbow trout fillets

2 T. fresh lemon juice

1 tsp. dillweed

1 tsp. salt

$^1/_4$ tsp. white pepper

1 pint whipping cream

2 T. dried bread crumbs

Wash fish; pat dry. Brush inside and out with lemon juice. Sprinkle with dillweed, salt and pepper. Place in lightly buttered baking dish. Pour cream, then bread crumbs, on top. Bake at 400 degrees for 15 minutes or until fish flakes easily with fork.

Benjamin Williams
Longview, TX

68

Salmon Casserole

1 pkg. long grain and wild rice mix

Butter

2-3 lbs. salmon, filleted

Lemon, cut into wedges

Parsley

Cook wild rice according to package directions. Coat inside of large casserole dish with butter. When rice is done, spread one-third of rice in bottom of casserole dish. Alternate layers of salmon fillet and rice mix; ending with layer of rice. Bake at 350 degrees for 1 hour or until salmon flakes easily. Serve with lemon wedges and parsley garnish.

Peter J. Houghton
Duanesburg, NY

Baked Smoked Salmon Fillet

¼ cup vegetable or olive oil

⅓-¼ cup hickory seasoned liquid smoke

Salt

Lemon pepper

1 salmon fillet

Line cookie sheet with doubled over aluminum foil. Combine oil, liquid smoke, salt and lemon pepper in pan. Marinate fish meat side up in mixture for 15-30 minutes. Pour off marinade. Roll up fish tightly in foil. Bake at 350 degrees for 30 minutes. Note: If fish is more than 1-inch thick, add 15-20 minutes cooking time.

Lealand Haybarker
Thorn Bay, AK

Orange Almond Trout

Orange Almond Trout

¼ cup sliced almonds

1 medium onion, sliced

¼ cup margarine

½ cup flour

1 tsp. salt

½ tsp. paprika

⅛ tsp. pepper

1 lb. trout fillets

2 oranges, pared, sectioned

Cook and stir almonds, onions and margarine in skillet until onions are tender. Remove with slotted spoon; keep warm. Mix flour, salt, paprika and pepper. Coat fish with flour mixture. Cook fish in same skillet over medium heat, turning carefully until brown, about 10 minutes. Top with almonds and onion; garnish with orange sections.

Tim Gizynski
Chicago, IL

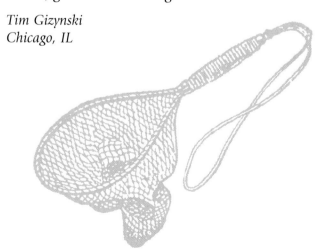

Salmon Loaf with Creamy Dill Sauce

Fish:

Salmon

1 cup frozen peas

½ cup diced onion

½ cup diced celery

¼ tsp. dried dill

1 cup crushed bran flakes cereal

3 eggs, lightly beaten

3 T. white vinegar

Dill Sauce:

½ cup cottage cheese

¼ cup lowfat plain yogurt

⅛ tsp. dried rubbed dill

Grease and wax paper line 8 x 4-inch loaf pan. Crush or remove bones from salmon; flake. Add remaining ingredients; mix well. Pack into prepared loaf pan. Bake at 350 degrees for 70 minutes. Let stand 10 minutes; turn out and slice. Serve with dill sauce.

To prepare dill sauce, combine all ingredients in blender. Blend until smooth.

Leo G. J. Seffelaar
Broadview, Saskatchewan, Canada

Herb Mustard Salmon

Sauce:

2 T. butter

2 T. Dijon mustard

1 T. honey

1 T. lemon juice

$\frac{1}{2}$ tsp. dried tarragon leaves

2 green onions, finely chopped

Freshly ground black pepper

Fish:

4 salmon steaks

1 green onion, finely chopped

1 T. chopped fresh parsley or dill

$\frac{1}{2}$ cup dry white wine

Baked Sandtrout with Lime Tarragon Butter

7-8 sandtrout fillets

Olive oil

1 stick butter

Juice of 1 lime

1 tsp. tarragon

Rub fillets with olive oil. Melt butter; add lime juice and tarragon. Baste fish frequently with mixture while baking at 375 degrees for 6-7 minutes per pound, until done. Serve with butter drizzled over fish.

Jack D. Hunter
Harlingen, TX

Prepare sauce by melting butter in small microwaveable bowl. Stir in remaining sauce ingredients until smooth. Set aside. Place salmon steaks in single layer in shallow microwaveable dish. Sprinkle with green onion and parsley. Pour wine over salmon; cover with vented plastic wrap. Microwave at high for 6-8 minutes. Rotate dish part way through cooking. Let stand 3 minutes. Place salmon steaks on individual plates; serve with sauce.

Leo G. J. Seffelaar
Broadview, Saskatchewan, Canada

Elegant Grilled and Stuffed Salmon

Marinate fish in lemon pepper marinade overnight. To prepare stuffing mixture, sauté garlic, onion and crab in margarine until vegetables are translucent. Add to prepared stuffing mix. Remove fish from marinade. Arrange fillets in fish grilling basket. Grill over hot coals until fish flakes. Remove fillets from basket; place in 9 x 13-inch baking pan. Place layer of stuffing mixture on fillet. Cover with another fillet. Repeat as needed until all fillets are sandwiched with stuffing mixture.

To prepare white sauce, melt butter in microwave. Add flour and salt; blend into smooth paste. Stir wine into paste; microwave on high for 2 minutes. Remove from microwave and add milk, stirring until blended. Microwave on high for 2 minutes, stir at 30-second intervals. When sauce is thickened and smooth, ladle over all stuffed fillets. Bake at 350 degrees for 15 minutes or until heated throughout.

Harvey Miller
Ludington, MI

Fish:

*3-5 lbs. salmon steaks
(skinned, filleted)*

Lemon pepper marinade

Stuffing Mixture:

1 large clove garlic, minced

1 small onion, finely chopped

8 oz. imitation crab meat

3 T. margarine

*1 pkg. stuffing mix,
prepared as directed*

White Sauce:

2 T. butter

2 T. flour

$1/2$ tsp. salt

$1/4$ cup white wine

$3/4$ cup milk

73

Festive Salmon Steaks

Sprinkle both sides of salmon with salt and pepper. Place in buttered baking dish large enough to hold steaks in single layer. Sprinkle with onion and tarragon. Pour champagne over salmon. Bake, covered, at 400 degrees for 20-30 minutes. Pour off cooking liquid into measuring cup. Add more champagne, if necessary, to make 1 cup liquid. Keep salmon warm. Melt butter in medium saucepan. Stir in cornstarch; cook until bubbly. Remove from heat. Gradually blend in fish liquid. Cook, stirring, until mixture boils. In a separate bowl, beat egg yolks with cream and mustard. Mix in small amount of warm sauce. Without heat, smoothly blend egg mixture into remaining sauce. Cook over low heat until thickened, stirring constantly (do not boil). Serve salmon steaks with sauce spooned over. Sprinkle with parsley. Garnish with lime slices.

Benjamin Williams
Longview, TX

4 salmon steaks

Salt

Pepper

1 green onion, finely chopped

¼ tsp. dried tarragon leaves

¾ cup extra dry champagne or white grape juice

2 T. butter

2 tsp. cornstarch

2 egg yolks

⅓ cup whipping cream

1 tsp. Dijon mustard

Parsley, chopped

Lime, sliced

Baked Salmon

Mayonnaise

Dried dill

4 salmon steaks

Lemon pepper

Spread mayonnaise on bottom of baking dish. Sprinkle with dill. Arrange salmon in dish; cover with mayonnaise. Sprinkle with lemon pepper and dill. Bake for 20-30 minutes, until salmon is flaky.

James and Cindy Bell
Ft. Lewis, WA

Festive Salmon Steaks

Go Fish

1 tsp. dill

1 tsp. onion

1 tsp. thyme

1 tsp. sweet basil

1 tsp. garlic

1 tsp. lemon pepper

1 tsp. rosemary

1 tsp. salt

1 tsp. parsley

Trout, whole, cleaned

Margarine

Combine all spices together. Sprinkle spices inside and outside of whole fish. Place 1 teaspoon margarine inside fish. Wrap fish in foil. Bake at 350 degrees for 20 minutes.

John Hopkins
Rescue, CA

Baked Trout with Herbs

4 trout, cleaned

Vegetable oil

Juice of 1 lemon

Salt

Pepper

4 T. chopped parsley

4 T. chopped chives

4 T. chopped dill

4 T. butter

Lemon, sliced

Fresh dill or parsley

Cut 4 pieces of aluminum foil large enough to completely enclose each trout. Rub trout lightly with oil and lemon juice. Sprinkle with salt and pepper. Place each trout on piece of foil. Top each with 1 tablespoon parsley, 1 tablespoon chives, 1 tablespoon dill and 1 tablespoon butter. Fold foil to seal trout. Bake at 375 degrees for 25 minutes. Remove fish from foil. Transfer to preheated plate. Garnish with lemon slices and fresh dill; serve immediately.

Benjamin Williams
Longview, TX

Fried Trout

2 tsp. butter, melted

Oregano

2 trout, cleaned, heads cut off

Place teaspoon of butter and dash of oregano inside each trout. Melt butter in hot skillet. Add fish; fry until fish are flaky and skin falls off. Drain fat.

Daniel Ludwig
New Holland, PA

Rocky Mountain Trout

Beer

Trout fillets

Salt

Pepper

Dried dillweed

Onion, diced

Fill skillet half full of beer. Sprinkle fillets with salt, pepper and dillweed. Place fillets in skillet; add onions. Add water to skillet until fish are covered. Heat to medium-high heat until beer begins to simmer. Cook until fish can be pulled apart with fork.

Lee Tripp
Colorado Springs, CO

Salmon Steaks Oriental

$1/2$ cup butter

2 T. chopped gingerroot

1 clove garlic, finely chopped

$1/4$ cup lime juice

1 T. soy sauce

1 tsp. Dijon mustard

1 tsp. peanut or sesame oil

1 tsp. brown sugar

Pinch of cayenne pepper

4 salmon steaks

Sesame seeds, toasted

Heat butter in skillet. Sauté ginger and garlic until golden. Stir in lime juice, soy sauce, mustard, oil, brown sugar and cayenne. Place salmon in single layer in greased baking dish. Pour sauce over fish. Cover with foil. Bake at 425 degrees for 10-12 minutes per inch thickness of fish. Sprinkle liberally with sesame seeds just before serving.

Leo G. J. Seffelaar
Broadview,
Saskatchewan,
Canada

Tortilla Crusted Salmon

2 T. Creole seasoning

Seasonings of choice

Salmon, sliced into 1-inch fillets

2 cups flour

1 egg

1½ cups milk

2 red corn tortillas, sliced into thin strips

2 yellow corn tortillas, sliced into thin strips

2 white corn tortillas, sliced into thin strips

Oil

Season fish; dredge in flour. Whip egg and milk together. Dip fish in eggwash; press tortilla strips on to fish. Sauté with oil for 3 minutes per side at medium heat. Tortillas should be brown and crisp, not burned.

James Didier II
New Orleans, LA

Grilled Mexican Trout

8-oz. jar salsa

Juice of 1 lime

4 trout, filleted

Mix salsa and lime juice; set aside. Grease grill thoroughly. Grill trout over hot coals for 5 minutes. Flip trout, spread salsa over fish; grill 5-7 more minutes or until fish flakes.

James and Cindy Bell
Ft. Lewis, WA

Grilled Mexican Trout

Tasty Trout

1/4 lb. butter, melted

Whole trout, cleaned with head, tail, skin on

2-3 lemon wedges

1/8 tsp. garlic salt

1/8 tsp. pepper

1/2 tsp. thyme

Kale leaf

Heat butter in saucepan until mildly boiling for 3-5 minutes. Place fish on aluminum foil. Insert as many lemon wedges as possible inside fish. Sprinkle with garlic salt, pepper and thyme. Pour butter into fish; wrap and seal tightly in foil. Bake at 350 degrees for 35-40 minutes or until meat falls off bones. Garnish with kale leaf.

Wyatt and Michelle Connolly
Layton, UT

Salmon Miso Yaki

4 T. light miso

1 tsp. sugar

2 T. mirin or sherry

1 T. olive oil

1 T. grated fresh ginger

1 salmon fillet or 4 salmon steaks

Gently warm miso, sugar, mirin, oil and ginger in saucepan. Cut salmon fillet or steaks into four serving pieces. Place in oiled foil-lined baking sheet. Bake at 400 degrees for 5 minutes. Turn oven to broil. Remove salmon. Brush miso mixture on salmon. Broil until lightly browned, about 1-2 minutes.

Leo G. J. Seffelaar
Broadview, Saskatchewan, Canada

Jim's Fish Loaf

2 pkg. unflavored gelatin

1/2 cup cold water

1 can condensed tomato soup
(undiluted)

8-oz. pkg. cream cheese, softened

1 cup finely chopped celery

1 cup finely chopped red
and green bell peppers

12 oz. trout or salmon, deboned,
cooked, cut up

1 cup mayonnaise

1 T. grated onion

1 T. horseradish

1 T. finely chopped, drained capers

1/2 tsp. bottled hot sauce

Salt

Dissolve gelatin in cold water. Heat toma-to soup; boil. Add gelatin; mix well. Cook until barely warm. Add cream cheese; mix well. Add remaining ingredients; mix well. Pour mixture into greased mousse mold, Bundt pan or 9 x 5-inch loaf pan. Cover; chill until set, about 2-4 hours. Unmold loaf onto large platter. Serve with vegetables, crackers or toast.

Jim Fain
Susanville, CA

Steamed Trout and Chives

3 whole trout

Oil

3 T. minced fresh chives

Additional chopped chives

Rub trout cavities with oil; stuff trout with chives. Place fish in steamer. Steam for 15 minutes. Remove chives; fillet trout. Top with fresh chives.

James and Cindy Bell
Ft. Lewis, WA

Top Trout

1 cup olive oil

1 tsp. oregano

1/4 tsp. cayenne pepper
(optional)

4 whole trout, cleaned

4 tsp. butter

Combine olive oil and spices. Baste trout in sauce. Place on hot grill. Cook 4-6 minutes, depending on thickness of trout. Melt butter; drizzle over fish before serving.

Shane Felber
Kankakee, IL

Crusty Corn Trout

Crusty Corn Trout

4 trout, cleaned, boned

$1/3$ cup flour

1 egg, beaten

1 T. lemon juice

1 cup yellow cornmeal

$1/4$ cup ground walnuts or pecans

1 tsp. salt

$1/4$ tsp. cracked pepper

$1/4$ tsp. paprika

$1/4$ tsp. cumin

Vegetable oil

Roll trout in flour. Beat egg with lemon juice. Mix cornmeal, nuts, salt, pepper, paprika and cumin. Dip floured trout into egg; then cornmeal mixture. Heat oil in skillet to medium. Cook trout, turning once, until both sides are brown; about 5 minutes per side.

Phillip G. Epping
Neillsville, WI

Fried Brook Trout

4-6 trout, cleaned
with head and tail on

3 T. flour

Salt

1 T. oil

1 stick butter

Juice of 1 lemon

1 clove garlic

4 T. minced chives

Dust trout with flour and salt. Heat oil and half the butter in skillet. Cook fish 3-4 minutes on each side (depending on size). Melt remaining butter; combine with lemon juice, garlic and chives in small skillet. Pour over fish. Serve with rice.

Lissa and Eddie Munoz
Oxnard, CA

83

Salmon Tartar

1½ lbs. salmon fillets,
chopped fine

½ lb. smoked salmon,
chopped fine

1 bunch Italian parsley,
rinsed, chopped

8 anchovy fillets, roughly chopped

8 T. chopped shallots

6 T. capers

2 T. horseradish

4 T. Dijon or whole grain mustard

Juice of 3 lemons

Tabasco

Salt

Pepper

Combine all ingredients; let stand for 2 hours in refrigerator. Serve with sliced French bread or crackers.

Karl Ulmer
Hawley, PA

Whole BBQ Salmon with Cucumber Dill Sauce

Fish:

1 whole salmon, dressed

1 orange, sliced

1 lemon, sliced

1 cup chopped fresh dill

Cucumber Dill Sauce:

6-oz. container plain yogurt

1 medium cucumber, peeled, chopped

1 tsp. fresh dill

1 tsp. brown sugar

½ tsp. salt

¼ tsp. pepper

½ tsp. Tabasco sauce

Stuff salmon with orange slices, lemon slices and half of dill. Set aside 1 teaspoon of dill for sauce. Sprinkle rest of dill around outside of salmon. Double wrap salmon in aluminum foil. Place on hot barbecue grill. Turn occasionally. When foil wrap pops up, salmon is done. To prepare cucumber dill sauce, combine all sauce ingredients. Serve with cooked salmon.

Leo G. J. Seffelaar
Broadview, Saskatchewan, Canada

Baked Teriyaki Salmon

4 pieces salmon, 1-inch thick

1 bottle teriyaki sauce

1 can crushed pineapple

Place salmon in baking dish. Pour most of teriyaki sauce on fish; soak for 2-3 hours. Spread pineapple over fish. Pour balance of teriyaki sauce on fish. Soak for another 30 minutes. Cover dish; place in oven. Bake at 350 degrees for 30-45 minutes.

Jack Allen
Mancelona, MI

Poached Salmon

Whole salmon

1 liter 7 Up

1 cup peppercorns

Lemon, sliced

Onion, sliced

Place salmon in Dutch oven with cover. Fill with 7 Up and peppercorns. Layer top of salmon with lemon and onion slices. Cover; cook until fish flakes easily.

Mike Evangelista
Arlington Heights, IL

The Only BBQ Salmon

8 large cloves garlic, finely chopped

1 tsp. salt

4 T. finely chopped parsley

2 T. finely minced sun-dried tomatoes

1/4 cup olive oil

1 salmon fillet

Sprinkle garlic with salt; grind together with flat of knife. Combine with parsley, tomatoes and olive oil. Store, covered in refrigerator overnight. Oil barbecue grill to prevent sticking. Cut two lengthwise slits in salmon fillet; cut to skin (not through). Spread half garlic mixture over fillet and into slits. Place skin side down on grill at low temperature. Barbecue for 10-15 minutes. Spread remaining garlic mixture over fillet. Increase grill temperature to medium; cook another 15 minutes until flesh separates into natural sections when pressed with fork.

Leo G. J. Seffelaar
Broadview, Saskatchewan, Canada

WALLEYE

Where they swim, walleye are a popular

gamefish—in no small part because they

are also a delicious tradition on the table.

Walleye meat is mild and fine-textured,

and suited for many types of cooking.

Good, gentle spicing brings out

the great flavor. NAFC members know

what makes walleye good, as you'll see

in the recipes that follow.

Walleye Stir-Fry

Vegetable oil

*1 lb. walleye, cut in
1-inch strips*

1 lb. stir-fry mixed vegetables

1 small can water chestnuts

1 cup pineapple chunks

1 T. Worcestershire sauce

1 T. soy sauce

10 drops jalapeño sauce (optional)

1 cup sweet and sour mix

Place vegetable oil in skillet. Fry fish until half done. Add rest of ingredients; cook until vegetables are tender. Serve from skillet.

*Ray E. Mellott
Findlay, OH*

Miracle Walleye

Mayonnaise

Walleye fillets

Ritz crackers, crushed

Parmesan cheese

Rub mayonnaise over fish. Combine crackers and Parmesan cheese. Roll fish in cracker mixture. Spray grill with nonstick spray or oil. Place fillets on grill. Cook about 15 minutes or until done.

*John W. Rhoades
Westlake, OH*

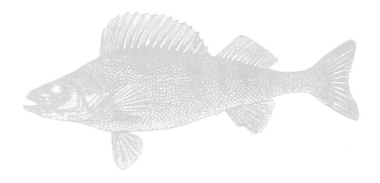

Walleye Stir-Fry

New Walleye Recipe

Walleye fillets

Butter

1 can stewed tomatoes

Campfire Delight

5 medium potatoes, chopped

4 white onions, chopped

4 walleye fillets, cubed

3 T. seasoned salt

1 T. black pepper

8-12 T. butter

Double over sheet of aluminum foil. Place fillets on foil; under each fillet place one tablespoon of butter. Spoon tomatoes over fillets. Make "tent" out of foil; crimp edges to secure and seal foil around fillets. Place foil on grill or coals. Cook for about 15-20 minutes or until done. Unwrap foil so as not to let juices escape. Place fresh bread slice on plate. Scoop melted butter, tomatoes and fish onto bread. Serve with home-fried potatoes.

Glen Dunn
Rolling Meadows, IL

Place potatoes, onions and walleye in large bowl. Add seasoned salt and black pepper. Lay out 4 pieces of 18-inch foil. In center of each foil piece, place one-fourth of walleye mixture. Add 2-3 tablespoons butter to each mixture. Seal fish mixture in foil; double wrap with second piece of foil seam-side down. Cook on grill for about 30 minutes or until done.

Michael and Aimee Saindon
Helena, MT

Easy Walleye

4 walleye fillets

1 egg, beaten

1 cup crushed cornflakes

Oil

Salt

Pepper

Dip fillets in egg. Press walleye into cornflakes. Heat oil in skillet; fry fish in hot oil until golden brown. Salt and pepper to taste.

Ray Rohde
Fargo, ND

My Favorite Walleye

Walleye, skin removed, cut into slabs

Lemon pepper

Butter

Sprinkle walleye with lemon pepper. Pan-fry in butter.

Chuck Figgins
Cedar Creek, MO

Eric's Walleye Recipe

1 walleye fillet

$^1/_4$ stick butter

Lemon pepper

Onions, chopped

Place fillet on sheet of aluminum foil. Add butter, lemon pepper and onions. Wrap foil around fillet. Heat grill. Place fish on grill. Cook about 15 minutes or until done.

Eric Milas
Gilman, WI

Fish Sandwich
with Roasted Red Peppers

Fish Sandwich with Roasted Red Peppers

To make red pepper sauce, combine mayonnaise, ketchup and hot sauce. Stir. Blend in remaining ingredients. Chill 1 hour. To make sandwiches, mix bread crumbs and Cajun seasoning. Beat eggs in separate bowl. Dip fillets in flour, then eggs. Cover fillets with seasoned bread crumbs. Fry fillets in oil until golden brown. Cut rolls; fill with shredded lettuce and tomatoes. Place fish pieces on rolls; drizzle with red pepper sauce. Garnish with chopped tomatoes, onions and cayenne pepper. Serve with pasta salad.

Rob Wodzinski
Iron River, MI

Walleye Recipe

Lemon pepper

Garlic powder

Walleye fillets

Butter

Hot sauce

Sprinkle lemon pepper and garlic powder on both sides of fillets. Melt butter and hot sauce in saucepan. Spray grill with nonstick cooking spray or oil. Place fish on grill. Baste with butter mixture throughout cooking process until fish is done; about 15 minutes.

John W. Rhoades
Westlake, OH

Red Pepper Sauce:

$^1/_2$ cup mayonnaise

$^1/_4$ cup ketchup

$^1/_2$ T. hot sauce

1 T. whole yellow mustard seed

1 T. celery seed

$^1/_2$ cup chopped red peppers

$^1/_4$ cup chopped onions

$^1/_4$ tsp. Cajun seasoning

Sandwich:

1 cup bread crumbs

2 T. Cajun seasoning

2 large eggs

4 walleye fillets, cut into 3-inch strips

Flour

2-3 cups vegetable oil

4 hard sandwich rolls, cut into 8-inch sections

2 cups shredded lettuce

2 tomatoes, chopped

2 onions, chopped

Cayenne pepper

FAVORITE FISH

Many recipes don't specify an exact fish

species to use. Rather, these fish traditions

are so tried-and-true, and universally good,

that they work with most any fish. It may be

your favorite fish, it may just be what

you ended up catching, it may be what's

in your freezer ... no matter what

the fish, you will find some

new favorite recipes here.

Fish Chowder

6 large potatoes, diced

1 large onion, diced

1-2 carrots, grated

1-2 stalks celery, chopped

2 T. butter

3-4 cups diced fish

6 cups milk

Salt

Pepper

Boil potatoes in large pot until tender. Drain; set aside. Sauté onions, carrots and celery in butter until tender. Add fish, milk, butter, celery, onions and carrots to potatoes. Cook until fish is done, stirring frequently to keep from sticking. Salt and pepper to taste.

Richard Hutcheson
Texarkana, TX

Fish Soup

2 lbs. fish

1 medium onion, chopped

Dash of pepper

Dash of salt

2 dashes Greek seasoning

2 dashes garlic powder

1 T. butter

2 cups milk

4 T. flour

2 cans cream of mushroom soup

2 cans cream of celery soup

3 cans cream of potato soup

Boil fish. Remove flesh from bone. Combine fish and onions. Cook over low heat. Add pepper, salt, seasoning, garlic and butter. Cook until onions are tender. Add other ingredients until heated through.

James Duncan
Aiken, SC

Fish Stew

Salt

Pepper

4 lbs. white fish

Oil

3 sweet onions, sliced

2 slices bacon, chopped

6 cups water

1 cup diced carrots

1 cup diced turnips

1 papaya, sliced, par-boiled

1 T. chopped parsley

1 sprig thyme

5 large potatoes, diced

1 can tomato paste

4 T. butter

Sprinkle fish with salt and pepper; brown in skillet with hot oil. Remove fish; brown onions and bacon. Place fish, onions and bacon in large saucepan. Add water; boil. Add vegetables and thyme. Cook until fish and vegetables are tender. When cooked, add tomato paste and butter. Salt to taste. Serve with rice.

Mr. Roy J. Timberlake
Buffalo, NY

Steamed Fish

Small finger fresh gingerroot

1 whole fish

$^1/_2$ cup peanut oil

4 green onions, chopped

2 tsp. soy sauce

3 T. oyster flavored sauce

Sugar

$^1/_2$ cup Chinese parsley

In saucepan, place $^1/_2$-inch water with piece of gingerroot. Boil water. Place fish in pot; steam for 10-15 minutes. Pour oil in skillet; heat until smoking. Place fish in deep dish; sprinkle green onion on top. Mix soy sauce, oyster sauce and sugar. Pour mixture over fish and onion. Pour hot peanut oil over green onion and sauce. Serve at once after the oil is poured on fish. Garnish with parsley.

Moi Hunter
Hilo, HI

Fish Recipe

2 eggs

¹/₄ cup milk

1 cup flour

¹/₂ cup cornmeal

¹/₂ tsp. curry powder

¹/₄ tsp. garlic powder

Salt

Pepper

Oil

Whip eggs while adding milk to blend. In separate bowl, combine dry ingredients. Pour enough oil in skillet to cover bottom. Heat oil. Dip fish in egg mixture, then in dry mixture. Place fish in hot skillet. Fry 2-3 minutes per side.

Barbara Rabold
Dayton, OH

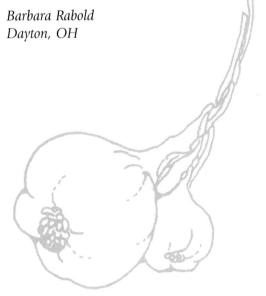

Creole Fillets

1 cup chopped onion

1 cup chopped green pepper

1 clove garlic, minced

3 T. oil

2 lb. can tomatoes, diced

1 or 2 bay leaves

1¹/₂ tsp. salt

Dash white, red or cayenne pepper

2 lbs. fish fillets

Cook onion, green pepper and garlic in oil until tender. Add tomatoes, bay leaf, salt and pepper. Simmer 30 minutes. Place fish in 11 x 7 x 2-inch baking pan. Sprinkle with salt and pepper. Pour tomato mixture over fish. Bake at 350 degrees for 45 minutes.

William Adams
Cahokia, IL

Creole Fillets

Fish Chowder

Prepare sherry pepper sauce by combining sherry and hot peppers. Put in bottle; set aside. Simmer fish in water with salt, pepper, thyme, bay leaves, peppercorns, ground cloves and garlic. In skillet, sauté onions, celery, garlic and green peppers. Add crushed tomatoes and consommé. Simmer 30 minutes. Add fish, ketchup, parsley, Worcestershire, lemon juice, potatoes, carrots, dark rum and sherry pepper juice. Cook for 3½ hours. Put fish in pot of water and spices. Boil until fish flakes. Strain fish in strainer. Flake fish back unto broth; discard spices. To make thicker broth, remove half of broth, blend and return to pot.

Roy J. Timberlake
Buffalo, NY

1 cup sherry

6 small hot peppers

4-6 medium fish fillets

4 qts. water

Salt

Pepper

Thyme

Bay leaves

Peppercorns

Ground cloves

Garlic

3 large onions, chopped

8 stalks celery, chopped

1 clove garlic, crushed

2 green peppers, chopped

1-lb. crushed tomatoes

10-oz. can consommé

1 cup ketchup

8 sprigs parsley

2 T. Worcestershire sauce

2 T. lemon juice

2 lbs. potatoes, peeled, diced

6 carrots, chopped

Dark rum

Pickled Fish

2 qts. fish

2 cups cider vinegar

$^1/_2$ cup salt

1 T. pickling spices

2 cups sugar

1 pinch cinnamon

$^1/_4$ tsp. coarse black pepper

1 T. dillweed

2 cups white vinegar

$^1/_2$ cup white wine

1 large onion, chopped

3 whole cloves

1 lemon, sliced into rounds

2 hot peppers, cut into rings

Fish in Beer Batter

$1^1/_2$ cups Jiffy Mix

$^3/_4$ cup beer

1 egg

$^1/_4$ tsp. salt

Pepper

4 fresh fish, pan-dressed

Oil

Place fish pieces, cider vinegar and salt in large bowl. Fish should be completely covered in solution. Put in refrigerator for 5-6 days. Pour out brine solution. Soak in pickling spices, sugar, cinnamon, black pepper, dillweed and white vinegar. Simmer on low for 5 minutes. When cool, add white wine. Place fish in small pint jars. Mix in onions, cloves, lemons and hot peppers. Pour juices over fish; tighten lids on jars. Place in refrigerator for 8 days.

Rob Wodzinski
Iron River, MI

Combine Jiffy Mix, beer, egg, salt and pepper; mix well. Dry fish; dip in batter. Fry in hot oil 4-5 minutes.

Ron and Becky Zirkel
Medora, IN

101

Fish on a Stick

Fish on a Stick

> Lemon juice
>
> Fish fillets
>
> Seasoning of choice: paprika, turmeric, seasoned salt, white pepper, lemon pepper, Cajun seasoning, etc.

Sprinkle lemon juice over fillets. Weave fillets on skewers in "s" shaped pattern. Sprinkle fillets with choice of seasonings. Place skewers under hot broiler or on grill. Cook until flaky.

Raymond S. Hodgson
Manito, IL

Fry Daddy Fish

> 5 cups flour
>
> 4 boxes Jiffy Corn Muffin mix
>
> Cornflakes, crushed
>
> Fresh fish fillets, chopped
>
> 1½ cups milk or diluted buttermilk
>
> Salt

Place 4 cups flour in large bag or container. In separate bag or container, place 1 cup flour, 4 boxes Jiffy Corn Muffin Mix and 3 cups crushed cornflakes. Place fillets in flour container; shake. Place on cookie sheet; set aside at room temperature for 15 minutes. Dip flour coated fillets into milk, then into Jiffy Corn Muffin mix container; shake well. Place fillets back on cookie sheet. Place in refrigerator for 30 minutes. Heat oil in skillet or deep fryer. Fry fish for 3-4½ minutes. Place on paper towels to drain. Salt to taste.

Wayne Moulin
Hollister, MO

Shore Lunch Fish Coating

1¹/₂ cups buttermilk
pancake mix

1 pkg. Italian salad dressing mix

2-3 fillets

Oil

Place dry ingredients in container with lid; shake. Place fillets in dry mixture; shake to coat. Immediately drop coated fillets in hot vegetable oil. Fry until golden brown.

Ed Dobberstein
Cumming, GA

Campfire Fish Dinner

1 fresh fish

2 slices bacon

1 potato, sliced

1 onion, sliced

Desired seasoning

Clean fish; lay out on piece of aluminum foil. Place slice of bacon on foil; place fish on bacon. Put potato and onion slices on fish; top with another piece of bacon. Season to taste. Seal fish in foil; cook in campfire coals for 20 minutes.

Scott Green
Salt Lake City, UT

Shake and Fry

2 cups crushed soda crackers

2 cups yellow cornmeal

2 cups flour

¹/₂ tsp. lemon pepper

1 egg

2 T. milk

Fish fillets

Oil

Combine crackers, cornmeal, flour and lemon pepper in paper sack. In bowl combine egg and milk. Place fillets in dry mixture sack; shake well to coat. Dip fillets in egg mixture. Return fillets to dry mixture; shake to coat. Heat oil in skillet; fry fillets until golden brown.

Cam Powers
Mason City, IA

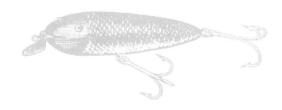

Sauce Baked Fish

¹/₂ stick margarine

4 T. Worcestershire sauce

4 T. soy sauce

1 T. seasoned salt

1-2 tsp. pepper

1 tsp. salt

1-2 tsp. seasoned pepper

Fish fillets

Melt margarine in skillet. Stir in remaining ingredients. Layer fillets in glass baking dish. Pour liquid mixture over fillets. Cover fish with aluminum foil. Bake at 350 degrees for 20 minutes. Remove foil and bake for 20 minutes more. Drain sauce off; bake for 5-10 more minutes.

Larry Boyer
Iowa Falls, IA

Stuffed Whitefish

3 lbs. whitefish, dressed, boned

Salt

¹/₄ cup chopped onion

3 T. chopped green pepper

1 T. butter

12-oz. can whole kernel corn, drained

1 cup soft bread crumbs

2 T. chopped canned pimento

¹/₈ tsp. crushed dried thyme

2 T. salad oil

Sprinkle inside of fish with salt. Place in well-greased shallow pan. Cook onion and pepper in butter. Stir in next 4 ingredients and ¹/₂ tsp. salt. Stuff fish loosely. Brush with oil; cover with foil. Bake at 350 degrees for 45-60 minutes.

Benjamin Williams
Longview, TX

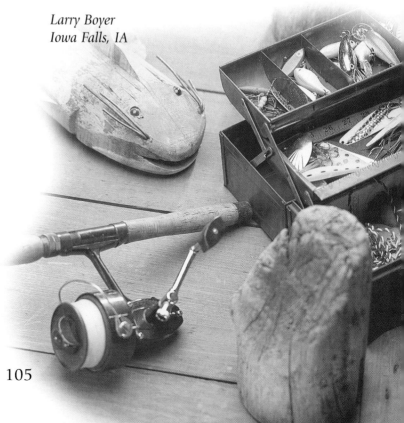

Pepito's Paella

In skillet, cook olive oil, chicken and pork. Near completion of cooking; add onions, garlic, pepper and parsley. Cook until ingredients stick slightly to pan. Remove these ingredients; will be added back in later. Add wine and broth to pan; mix. Add saffron to broth; mix. Add rice; stir slightly. Cover until rice boils; turn burner to low. Add cooked ingredients back into skillet, along with peas. When rice is almost cooked, decorate pan with shrimp and scallops in the center, mussels to the edge, crab and fish scattered throughout. If liquid is drying out, add more broth to create steam for mussels and seafood. Paella is complete when shrimp is pink, mussels are open, crab, fish, and scallops are white and rice is cooked. Salt and pepper to taste. Garnish with lemon and tomato.

William M. Pepito
Twin Lakes, WI

$1/3$ cup olive oil

1 lb. chicken breast, skinless, cubed

1 lb. pork, cubed

1 small onion, minced

3 cloves garlic, crushed

1 small bell pepper, chopped

3-5 T. minced fresh parsley

3 T. wine

4 cups chicken broth

Pinch of saffron

2 cups long grain rice

$3/4$ cup peas

$1/2$ lb. medium shrimp, peeled

$1/4$ lb. small sea scallops

1 lb. mussels

$1/2$ lb. crab meat or lobster meat

1 lb. favorite whitefish, chopped

Salt

Pepper

2 lemons, sliced into wedges

1 small tomato, chopped (optional)

Pepito's Paella

Lemon-Poached Whitefish

2 T. butter

2 lbs. whitefish fillets

2 large fresh lemons

Dash of pepper

Dash of dried mint

Dash of parsley

$1/4$ cup dry white wine

Melt butter in shallow baking dish. Place whitefish on butter. Squeeze lemons over fillets. Sprinkle pepper, mint and parsley over fillets. Add $1/4$ cup wine. Cover dish with foil. Bake at 350 degrees for 45 minutes.

David Baxter
Ayton, Ontario, Canada

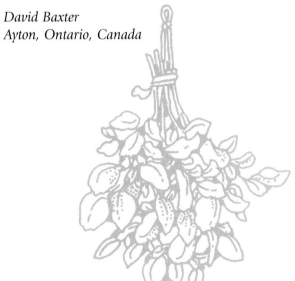

Batter Dip Fish

2 cups drake batter mix

$1/2$ tsp. paprika

$1/2$ tsp. parsley

$1/2$ tsp. basil

$1/2$ tsp. crushed tarragon

$1/2$ tsp. salt

$1/2$ tsp. pepper

3 eggs

1 can beer

Fish fillets

Oil

Combine dry ingredients. In separate bowl, beat eggs and beer. Dip fillets in egg mixture; then batter mixture. Heat oil in skillet; fry until golden brown.

Thomas Azbell
Lancaster, OH

Baked Fish with Mushroom Stuffing

To prepare mushroom stuffing, put butter in a saucepan. Add onions; sauté until golden, but not brown. Add mushrooms; cook until water from mushrooms evaporates. Remove from heat. Add bread crumbs, chicken stock, egg, 1/2 teaspoon salt and pepper. Mix with hands.

To clean fish, rub inside with 1 teaspoon salt. Stuff fish with mushroom stuffing. Fasten with skewers or toothpicks; place belly down in greased baking dish. Layer bacon over fish. Bake at 350 degrees for 1 hour or until fish flakes easily. Remove to preheated platter; garnish with lemon slices.

Paul H. Wells
Sierra Vista, AZ

Shore Lunch

2 fish fillets

1 can sliced potatoes

1 can stewed tomatoes

1 onion, sliced

Salt

Pepper

Desired seasonings

Mushroom Stuffing:

3 T. butter

1 small onion, chopped fine

1/2 cup chopped fresh mushrooms

2 cups dried bread crumbs

3/4 cup chicken stock

1 egg, beaten

1/2 tsp. salt

1/4 tsp. pepper

Fish:

3-4 lbs. whole fish, dressed

1 tsp. salt

4 strips bacon

Lemon slices

Place 1 fillet on sheet of heavy-duty aluminum foil. Pour potatoes, tomatoes and onion over fillets. Season with salt, pepper and any other desired seasonings. Top with other fillet; seal tightly. Place on grill. Cook about 10 minutes per side.

William J. Minta
Mukwonago, WI

109

Fish Patties

Fish Patties

2 lbs. boneless fillets, flaked

3 eggs

1 T. cooking sherry

1 T. Worcestershire sauce

1 tsp. sesame oil

1 cup chopped onion

2 cups crushed cornflakes

$^1/_2$ cup bread crumbs

Mix fish, 1 egg, wine, Worcestershire sauce, oil, onion and cornflakes. Form into patties. Beat remaining eggs in separate bowl. Dip patties in egg, then bread crumbs. Fry in $^1/_4$-inch oil until brown on both sides.

Herb Terry
Chickasha, OK

Baked Fish Fillets

2 lbs. fish fillets

$^1/_4$ tsp. paprika

3 T. lemon juice

Salt

Pepper

2 T. butter

2 T. flour

1 T. dry mustard

1 cup milk

$^1/_2$ cup buttered bread crumbs

1 T. minced parsley

Cut fillets into serving pieces. Place in greased shallow baking dish. Sprinkle with paprika, lemon juice, salt and pepper. Make white sauce by melting butter in pan; add flour, salt, pepper, mustard and milk. Cook quickly, stirring constantly until mixture thickens and bubbles. Remove from heat. Pour sauce over fillets. Sprinkle with bread crumbs and parsley. Bake at 350 degrees for 35 minutes.

William Adams
Cahokia, IL

Deep-Fried Fish and Potatoes

¹/₂ gallon oil

2 eggs

1¹/₂ cups flour

1 cup beer or water

Seasonings of choice

2 T. butter, melted

Fish fillets

Potatoes, sliced

Over open fire or stove, preheat cooking oil in deep pan or kettle until hot. Mix together eggs, flour, beer, seasonings and butter to make batter. Dip fillets in batter. Place battered fillets into hot oil. Fry until slightly brown before adding potato slices. Turn fillets and potatoes so they cook uniformly. Cook 8-10 minutes. Place on paper towels to drain.

Norma A. Blank
Shawano, WI

Fresh Fish Fillets

Fresh fish fillets

¹/₂ cup flour

¹/₂ cup cornmeal

1 tsp. salt

2 T. lemon butter seasoning

Oil

2 T. lemon juice

Wash fillets. Combine flour, cornmeal, salt and seasoning in bowl. Heat oil in skillet. Roll fillets in mixture, place in skillet, pour lemon juice over fillets and brown nicely. Add lemon butter seasoning to taste.

John P. Jones
Perry, OK

German Fish Casserole

1¹/₂ lbs. fish fillets, cut into
¹/₂-inch pieces

Juice of 1 lemon

Salt

Black pepper

2 tsp. paprika

1 tsp. butter

2 medium onions, finely chopped

3 sprigs parsley

1 lb. potatoes, peeled, sliced

3 eggs, lightly beaten

³/₄ cup sour cream

³/₄ cup yogurt

Sprinkle fillets with lemon juice, salt, pepper and paprika. Let sit 30 minutes. Sauté onion and parsley in butter until onion is transparent. Layer fish, onion and potatoes in greased casserole dish. Mix eggs, sour cream and yogurt in bowl. Pour mixture over casserole. Bake at 350 degrees, covered, for 30 minutes. Remove cover; bake 15 more minutes.

James and Cindy Bell
Ft. Lewis, WA

Fried Fish

2 tsp. garlic paste

2 tsp. tomato paste

1 medium onion paste

2 tsp. chili powder

2 tsp. lemon juice

2 tsp. pineapple juice

Salt

4 pieces fish, sliced

Oil

Romaine lettuce

2 tsp. chopped parsley or cilantro

Lime, finely sliced

Place garlic paste, tomato paste, onion paste, chili powder, lemon juice, pineapple juice and salt in bowl. Mix well. Place fish slices in bowl; mix well. Let sit 2 hours. Heat oil in large skillet. Fry fish in oil until golden brown. Remove fish from oil; drain on paper towels. Place fish on bed of lettuce; sprinkle parsley on top. Alternate lime slices and fish slices. Serve.

Note: If unable to find garlic, tomato or onion paste; make paste by using food processor to grind individual ingredient into paste.

Golam Faruque
Margate, FL

Fish Curry

4 tsp. canola oil

1 small onion, finely chopped

1 tsp. garlic

Salt

1/4 cup yogurt

1 tsp. chili powder

1 tsp. turmeric powder

1/2 tsp. ginger paste

1 tsp. ground coriander

1 tsp. ground cumin

2 medium tomatoes, sliced

Cinnamon

2 bay leaves

4 pieces fish, sliced

2 tsp. finely chopped cilantro

Herb-Baked Fish

1/2 onion, thinly sliced

1 lb. fish fillets

1 T. butter

1 tsp. salt

1/2 tsp. garlic salt

1/2 tsp. MSG (optional)

1/4 tsp. oregano

1/4 tsp. thyme

Dash of pepper

1 small bay leaf

1/2-3/4 cup light cream

Heat oil in skillet. Add onions, garlic and salt. Cook for 5-7 minutes. Add yogurt; cook for 5-7 more minutes. Add chili powder, turmeric powder, ginger paste, ground coriander, ground cumin, tomato slices, cinnamon and bay leaves. Cook for 10-15 minutes, until it turns to thick paste. Clean fish; pat dry. Place fillets in skillet. Cook 5-7 minutes in covered skillet; turn. Cook other side another 5-7 minutes. Garnish with cilantro; serve with rice.

Golam Faruque
Margate, FL

Separate sliced onions into rings. Place fish in 10 x 6 x 2-inch baking pan. Dot with butter; sprinkle with seasonings. Add bay leaf; arrange onion rings over top of fish. Pour cream over all. Bake for 40 minutes at 350 degrees.

William Adams
Cahokia, IL

Grilled Fish

Fish fillets

Butter

Lemon pepper seasoning

Seasoned salt

Garlic salt

Wash and pat dry fillets. Tear off piece of foil large enough for a few fillets. Place fillets on foil pieces. Dot each fillet with ¼ tablespoon butter. Sprinkle with desired amount of seasonings. Seal all edges of foil. Wrap in second sheet of foil. Place on grill for 20-30 minutes; turning as needed (about every 5 minutes).

Glen and Joyce Rodick
Bancroft, NE

Blackened Fish

1 tsp. sweet paprika

2½ tsp. salt

1 tsp. onion powder

1 tsp. garlic powder

1 tsp. cayenne pepper

¾ tsp. white pepper

¾ tsp. ground black pepper

½ tsp. dried thyme

½ tsp. dried oregano

Fresh fillets

Margarine, melted

Combine all spices together. Dip fillets in margarine; place on paper plate lined with foil or plastic wrap. Sprinkle both sides of fish with spice mixture. Heat skillet until very hot. Place fillets in pan. Fish should smoke and sizzle immediately. Cook for 1½ minutes per side. Turn fish once during cooking process.

Tom Huntowski
Minong, WI

Chas's Stuffed Fish

4 cups chopped bread
(including 1 slice seeded rye)

$^1/_2$ cup diced celery

$^1/_2$ cup diced onion

Fish (or chicken) broth

Salt

Pepper

Parsley

2 T. butter

4 trout, cleaned

Combine bread, celery and onion. Add broth; mix until bread is thoroughly moistened. Add salt, pepper and parsley to taste. Put $^1/_2$ tablespoon butter and one-fourth of stuffing in cavity of each fish. Put fish in baking pan; put extra stuffing in bottom of pan. Bake at 350 degrees for 45-60 minutes or until meat flakes away from bone.

Charles Van Noy
Titusville, NJ

Sweet Smoked Fish

1 cup brown sugar

1 cup white sugar

$^1/_2$ cup salt

1 tsp. garlic salt

1 tsp. black pepper

Fish fillets or steaks

1 T. honey

1 T. water

Combine sugars, salts and pepper together. Coat fillets with mixture. Place fish in air-tight plastic bag; refrigerate overnight. The night before smoking, soak hickory, mesquite or woods from fruit trees. Start coals. Take fish out of bag, rinse off extra salt and sugar. Place on greased grates to drain until coals are hot. Fill water pan; place fish in smoker for 2-4 hours or until fish flakes easily when fork-tested. About 30 minutes before fish are done, mix honey with water and brush fillets.

Richard Hutcheson
Texarkana, TX

Fish Fillets with Orange Sauce

1$^{1}/_{2}$ cups orange juice

2 T. lemon juice

$^{1}/_{2}$ cup dry white wine

$^{1}/_{2}$ tsp. dillweed

1 tsp. crushed garlic

$^{1}/_{2}$ tsp. salt

4-6 fillets

2 T. cornstarch

Green onion, chopped

Combine orange juice, lemon juice, wine, dillweed, garlic and salt. Mix well. Add fish fillets; marinate 2-4 hours, turning often. Remove fillets; set aside. Pour marinade into small saucepan, reserve $^{1}/_{4}$ cup. Boil marinade. Dissolve cornstarch in reserved marinade. Add to boiling marinade; stir until thickened. Broil fillets until flaky, turning once. Pour orange sauce over fillets. Serve with rice. Sprinkle with chopped green onion.

Jim Fain
Susanville, CA

Grilled Fish Fillet

2 tsp. chopped garlic

1 tsp. chili powder

$^{1}/_{2}$ tsp. freshly ground black pepper

2 tsp. lemon juice

$^{1}/_{2}$ tsp. sugar

$^{1}/_{2}$ tsp. cumin

$^{1}/_{4}$ cup balsamic vinegar

2 tsp. canola oil

Salt

4 fish fillets

Combine garlic, chili powder, pepper, lemon juice, sugar, cumin, vinegar, oil and salt in mixing bowl. Place fillets in bowl; mix well. Marinate for 20 minutes. Grill fillets on medium-hot grill. Garnish with parsley, tomato wedges, cucumber slices, lime slices and grated carrots.

Golam Faruque
Margate, FL

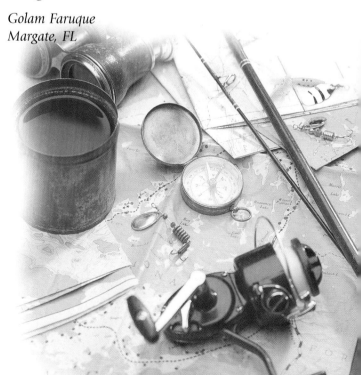

117

SALTWATER FISH

There are so many great
saltwater fish to eat—and even more
ways to prepare them. Here are some
of the fish-cooking traditions members
told us about—ideas for making
flounder, halibut, cod, tuna, mackerel,
cobia, grouper (and more) into
meals to remember.

Flounder
with Shrimp Sauce

Sprinkle flounder with lemon juice. Season with salt and black pepper. Dip fish in flour; shake off excess. Beat egg with fork. Dip floured fish into egg, then bread crumbs. Place fish on waxed paper; set aside. Combine shrimp in bowl with mayonnaise, chili sauce, curry powder and sherry. Add salt and pepper, if desired. Heat oil in heavy skillet. When hot, add fish a few at a time. Cook over medium heat for 3 minutes on each side. Serve on warm plate; garnish with dill or parsley and lemon wedges. Serve shrimp sauce on side.

Benjamin Williams
Longview, TX

Fish:

4 flounder, skin and head removed

Juice of 1 lemon

Salt

Black pepper

3 T. flour

1 egg

4 T. bread crumbs

Shrimp Sauce:

$^1/_2$ lb. small shrimp, cooked
or
1 (4$^1/_4$-oz.) can small shrimp, drained

1 cup mayonnaise

1 T. chili sauce

$^1/_8$ tsp. curry powder

1 T. sherry (optional)

6 T. oil

Fresh dill
or parsley

Lemon wedges

Cobia Fingers

1 egg, beaten

2 cups milk

*6-12 cobia fillets, cut into
1-inch strips*

2 cups hush puppy mix

Oil

Beat egg into milk. Place cobia strips into bowl. Pour mixture over strips. Dredge strips through hush puppy mix. Shake off excess. Pour oil into skillet. Fry strips for 3-5 minutes or until browned.

Patrick Bearden
Charlotte, NC

Cajun Halibut

1½ lbs. Pacific halibut steaks

1 cup finely chopped pecans

3 T. flour

½ tsp. salt

¼ tsp. pepper

2 T. maple syrup

4 T. salad oil

Pat halibut dry with paper towel. Mix together pecans, flour, salt and pepper on flat plate. With pastry brush, coat one side of each halibut steak with maple syrup. Dredge in pecan mixture. Repeat procedure to coat other side. Heat 2 tablespoons oil in skillet. Fry halibut at high heat for 10 minutes per inch thickness, turning once halfway through cooking. Add more oil to pan if necessary.

Leo G. J. Seffelaar
Broadview, Saskatchewan, Canada

Fish Soup

Fish:

1 lb. fresh cod fillets

3 T. lemon juice

1 T. salad oil

$1/2$ cup thinly sliced onion

$1/2$ cup sliced carrots

$1/2$ cup sliced celery

Soup:

19-oz. can tomatoes

$1/2$ cup noodles

4 cups water, boiled

1 T. salt

$1/2$ tsp. pepper

2 T. grated Parmesan cheese

Cut fish into serving-size portions. Sprinkle with lemon juice. Heat oil in saucepan; add onion, carrot and celery. Stir until thoroughly coated with oil. Cover; cook over low heat for 10 minutes. Add fish; simmer 10 minutes longer. Combine all soup ingredients except Parmesan cheese in saucepan; heat to boiling. Place fish in bowl; fill with soup. Sprinkle with grated Parmesan cheese.

Joyce Smith
Trinity Bay, Newfoundland, Canada

Halibut and Peppers Julienne

4-6 pacific halibut steaks

2 T. butter

1 red pepper, seeded,
cut into thin strips

1 green pepper, seeded,
cut into thin strips

$1/2$ yellow pepper, seeded,
cut into thin strips

1 onion, cut into thin strips

2 stalks celery, halved

1 tomato, seeded, coarsely chopped

1 tsp. chopped parsley

Dash paprika

Dash curry powder

Dash cayenne pepper

Dash salt

Dash pepper

$2/3$ cup white wine

Poach or steam halibut. Melt butter in skillet. Add vegetables and remaining ingredients, except halibut. Simmer 5 minutes. Spoon simmered vegetables and pan juices over halibut just before serving.

Leo G. Seffelaar
Broadview, Saskatchewan, Canada

Halibut and Peppers Julienne

Pacific Fish Lyonnaise

2 T. butter

4 small onions, thinly sliced

$^1/_2$ cup grated Parmesan cheese

$^1/_2$ cup fine bread crumbs

*1$^1/_2$ lbs. Pacific fish steaks
or fillets*

Salt

Freshly ground pepper

$^1/_2$ cup mayonnaise

Heat butter in skillet. Sauté onions 4-5 minutes until limp; set aside. Combine cheese and bread crumbs; set aside. Arrange fish portions on oiled rack of broiler pan. Season with salt and pepper. Spread half of mayonnaise over fish. Broil fish, placing them 4 inches from heat source, for 10 minutes per inch of thickness. Turn once, 3 minutes before end of cooking time. After turning, spread remaining mayonnaise and top with onion, cheese and crumb mixture.

Leo G. J. Seffelaar
Broadview, Saskatchewan, Canada

Barbecue Albacore Tuna

1 albacore tuna fillet

1 T. butter, melted

Garlic salt

Lemon pepper

Honey barbecue sauce

Wash and clean fillet. Brush melted butter on both sides of fillet. Sprinkle garlic salt and lemon pepper on both sides also. Place sheet of aluminum foil on hot grill. Lay fillet on foil. Baste fillet with honey barbecue sauce. Cook 5-7 minutes. Turn once, baste other side with barbecue sauce; cook 5-7 more minutes.

Earl Scarborough
Rialto, CA

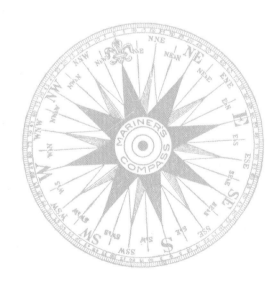

Dilly Fillets with Braised Celery

Fish:

1/2 tsp. crushed dill seed

1/4 tsp. celery seed

1/4 tsp. pepper

1/2 tsp. salt

1 1/2 lbs. cod fillets

2 T. butter

Braised Celery:

1 T. butter

4 stalks celery, diced

1/2 cup water

Parsley sprigs, chopped

Combine dill seed, celery seed, pepper and salt. Sprinkle over fish. Refrigerate fish, loosely covered for 1 hour. Place fish seasoned side up on greased broiler pan. Dot with 2 tablespoons butter. Broil for 10 minutes per inch of thickness at thickest part. Melt 1 tablespoon butter in medium-sized skillet. Add celery; toss to coat. Add water and parsley; cook over high heat, stirring constantly until water evaporates. Place cooked fish on serving platter; spoon celery over and around.

Leo G. J. Seffelaar
Broadview, Saskatchewan, Canada

Grilled Tuna

5 tuna steaks (about 6 oz. each)

12-oz. bottle Italian dressing

1 lemon

Place steaks in shallow baking pan. Pour dressing over steaks to marinate. Place in refrigerator for 3 hours. Grill over medium heat for 3-5 minutes per side. Squeeze lemon over steaks. Enjoy.

Patrick Bearden
Charlotte, NC

125

Quick Bouillabaisse

Quick Bouillabaisse

Rub toast with garlic clove. In large pan, heat oil and sauté garlic, onion and celery. Add herbs, spices, tomatoes, orange rind, stock, salt and pepper. Boil. Simmer 10-15 minutes. Add fish; cook for 2 minutes. Add clams, along with some clam juice. Simmer longer, until fish is cooked. Place slice of toast in bowls, spoon bouillabaisse on top.

Leo G. J. Seffelaar
Broadview, Saskatchewan, Canada

4-6 slices bread, toasted

2-4 cloves garlic, peeled

1 T. oil

1 large onion, sliced

1 celery stalk, minced

1/4 tsp. dried thyme

1/4 tsp. dried oregano

1 bay leaf

1/2 tsp. saffron or cumin powder

1 tsp. fennel seeds

14-oz. can tomatoes

1 tsp. grated orange rind

4 cups fish stock or chicken stock

Salt

Pepper

1/4 lb. semi-fatty fish fillets, cubed
(Arctic char, salmon)

1/2 lb. lean fish fillets, cubed
(sole, cod)

1/2 (14-oz.) can clams

Fried King Fish

2-3 fresh king fish, cleaned

$^1/_4$ tsp. salt

Pinch of pepper

$^3/_4$ cup flour

$^1/_8$ cup oil

1 lemon slice

Pat fish dry with paper towels. Combine salt, pepper and flour in flat plate. Heat oil in skillet until very hot. Roll each fish in flour mixture; place in hot skillet. Cook for 3 minutes per side or until done. Garnish with lemon.

Edna K. Hara
Los Angeles, CA

Cheese-It Baked Drum

$^1/_2$ cup butter

1 egg

4 T. grated Parmesan cheese

$^1/_2$ tsp. salt

$^1/_2$ tsp. pepper

$1^1/_2$ cups crushed Cheez-It crackers

1 tsp. parsley

6 puppy drum fillets

Melt butter in saucepan; allow to cool. Beat egg into butter. Mix all dry ingredients together in separate bowl. Drag fillets through butter; completely coat with cracker mixture. Lay fish in single layer in greased baking dish. Bake at 375 degrees for 25 minutes.

Patrick Bearden
Charlotte, NC

Cioppino

Pour oil into large saucepan. Add next 3 ingredients to saucepan; sauté until tender. Stir in next 13 ingredients (wine through lemon juice). Boil, cover, reduce heat and simmer 1 hour. Cool; cover and chill 12 hours. Pry off apron or tail flap from crabs. Lift off top shell, saving cream-colored "crab butter" from inside top shell; discard shell. Pull out and discard feathery gills adhering to body meat. Discard stomach mass; break crab into left and right sections. Twist legs and claws from body. Cut each body section crosswise into 2 pieces. Crack legs with wooden mallet. Set body pieces, cracked claws and "crab butter" aside. Discard any raw clams that are open. Warm chilled tomato mixture in large saucepan over medium heat, stirring occasionally, until thoroughly heated. Place crab, clams, shrimp and fish in large stockpot. Pour warm tomato broth over seafood; boil. Reduce heat, simmer 10-12 minutes. Discard any clams that did not open during cooking. Serve with sourdough bread; garnish with chopped fresh parsley.

J. Jones
San Diego, CA

¼ cup olive oil

2 onions, diced

6 garlic cloves, chopped

1 green bell pepper, chopped

2 cups dry red wine

2 cups clam juice

28-oz. can diced tomatoes

8-oz. can tomato sauce

1 bay leaf

1 T. sugar

1 T. dried oregano

1 T. dried basil

1 T. black pepper

1 T. dried, crushed red pepper

1 tsp. salt

¼ tsp. dried thyme

1 T. lemon juice

3 dungeness crabs, whole-cooked

1 lb. manila or
little-neck clams, scrubbed

1 lb. large fresh shrimp, unpeeled

3 lbs. Pacific rockfish fillets or other
white fish, cut into 1½-inch pieces

2 loaves sourdough bread

Fresh parsley, chopped

Halibut Portugesa

4 halibut steaks

Juice of $^1/_2$ lemon

2 medium tomatoes, peeled, chopped

1 medium onion, finely chopped

1 clove garlic, crushed

$^1/_2$ tsp. salt

1 tsp. sugar

$^1/_4$ cup chopped parsley

$^1/_4$ cup tomato paste

$^1/_4$ cup dry white wine

$^1/_4$ cup water

$^1/_2$ tsp. crushed (to powder) dried mint

4 thin slices lemon

1 T. butter

Place halibut in single layer in lightly buttered, shallow baking dish. Sprinkle with lemon juice. Combine tomato, onion and garlic in small saucepan. Simmer for 5 minutes. Add salt, sugar, parsley, tomato paste and wine; simmer until well blended. Stir in water and mint. Pour over fish. Lay lemon slices on top of fish; dot with butter. Cover dish with foil. Bake at 400 degrees for 15 minutes.

Leo Seffelaar
Broadview, Saskatchewan, Canada

Macadamia Nut Halibut

Garlic salt

1 halibut steak

1-1$^1/_2$ cups macadamia nuts

Sprinkle garlic salt on both sides of halibut steak. Place macadamia nuts in zip top plastic bag; crush with wooden mallet. Place crushed nuts in shallow dish. Place steak on nuts; press firmly. Turn once; press firmly again. Place steak in aluminum foil bag. Add favorite vegetables if desired. Cook on well-heated barbecue for 5-10 minutes.

Earl Scarborough
Rialto, CA

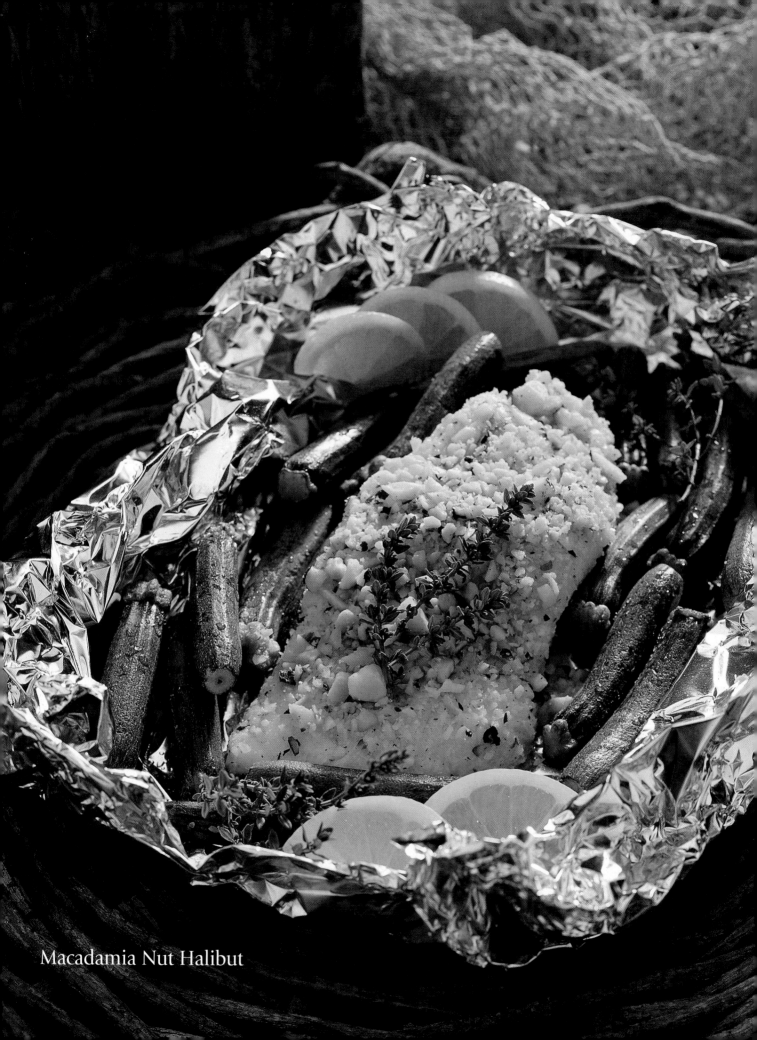

Macadamia Nut Halibut

Baked Scrod in Foil

6 scrod fillets

Salt

Freshly ground pepper

4 ripe plum tomatoes, seeded, slivered

1 red bell pepper, cored, seeded, slivered

1 small onion, peeled, halved, slivered

1 T. tiny capers, drained

6 tsp. chopped parsley

6 tsp. fresh lemon juice

2 T. extra virgin olive oil

Tear off 6 pieces of foil (14 x 12 inches). Center scrod fillets on lower half of each piece of foil. Sprinkle each fillet with salt and pepper. Arrange the vegetables equally on top of each piece of fish. Sprinkle evenly with capers and parsley. Drizzle each fillet with 1 teaspoon lemon juice and 1 teaspoon olive oil. Fold top half of foil over fish; seal on all sides. Place bundles on baking sheet. Bake at 400 degrees for 20 minutes.

Leslie J. Richardson
San Benito, TX

Fish in a Flash

1 lb. bluefish fillets

Juice of 1 lemon

Arrange fish in microwaveable dish. Sprinkle with lemon juice. Cover with plastic wrap. Poke holes in wrap to vent. Microwave 2 minutes. Turn fish, recover; microwave for 2 more minutes. Serve with hot rice.

James and Cindy Bell
Ft. Lewis, WA

Captain Ben's Crispy Cod

Fish:

1 lb. Pacific cod fillets, cut into bite-size pieces

$2/3$ cup cornstarch

$1/3$ cup flour

1 tsp. vinegar

Water

1 T. baking powder

Oil

Marinade:

2 T. soy sauce

1 T. chopped ginger

$1/8$ tsp. salt

$1/8$ tsp. pepper

Place cod pieces in bowl. Combine marinade ingredients; pour over cod. Stir. Set aside for 30 minutes, stirring and turning fish occasionally. Combine cornstarch, flour and vinegar. Add enough water to make medium-thick pancake batter. Add baking powder; stir. Dip marinated cod chunks in batter. Heat oil in deep fryer or skillet. Fry a few pieces at a time until golden brown.

Leo G. J. Seffelaar
Broadview, Saskatchewan, Canada

Bite-Size Albacore Tuna

1 T. margarine

3 T. mayonnaise

3 tsp. garlic salt

1 cup honey teriyaki barbecue sauce

2 albacore tuna, cut into bite-size pieces

Melt margarine in medium bowl. Add mayonnaise, garlic salt and barbecue sauce. Place tuna pieces into mixture; coat thoroughly. Place tuna in aluminum foil. Cook on grill for about 5 minutes or until done.

Earl J. Scarborough
Rialto, CA

Sunrise Surf Supreme

Sunrise Surf Supreme

Dip fillets into eggs. Combine cornstarch and mustard; coat both sides of fillets. Place fillets on foil lightly sprayed with nonstick spray. Spread 1 teaspoon chiles over each piece of fish. Bake at 350 degrees for 25 minutes. Prepare rice. Place rice on serving platter; add fish on top of rice. Garnish with tomatoes, avocado and basil leaves.

Richard Zablauskas
Bronx, NY

6-8 weakfish fillets

3-4 egg whites

1 cup cornstarch

2 T. dry mustard

1 jar mild green chile peppers, minced

1 pkg. rice pilaf

2 ripe tomatoes, cubed

1 avocado, cubed

Fresh basil leaves

Vegetable Cod

2 cups mini carrots, prepared

2 cups julienned parsnips

1 fennel bulb, chopped

Salt

Pepper

1 lb. cod

Onion

1 clove garlic, minced

1½ cups sliced mushrooms

2 tsp. butter

Boil vegetables in water for 5 minutes. Drain; reserve liquid. Puree half the vegetables with 1½ cups of cooking liquid. Season with fennel greens, salt and pepper. Poach fish in small quantity of cooking liquid for 5-7 minutes or until cooked. In skillet, sauté onion, garlic and mushrooms in butter. Spoon pureed vegetables on each plate. Add serving of fish on top, along with some remaining vegetables. Top with mushroom mixture. Serve with mashed potatoes.

Leo G. J. Seffelaar
Broadview, Saskatchewan,
Canada

Ocean Cod Bake

1½ lbs. cod fillets

1 cup dry white wine

½ cup seasoned bread crumbs

1 cup plain yogurt

¼ cup minced green onion

Paprika

Place fish in baking dish. Pour wine over cod; marinate in refrigerator 15-30 minutes. Discard wine; pat fish dry with paper towels. Dip both sides in bread crumbs. Place fish bake in baking dish. Combine yogurt and green onion; spread over fish. Sprinkle with paprika. Bake in 400-degree oven 15-20 minutes or until fish flakes when tested with fork.

Leslie J. Richardson
San Benito, TX

Seafood Salad

Place fish in glass baking dish. Cover loosely with waxed paper; microwave on high for 4-5 minutes. Let stand. Remove any skin and bones; cool to room temperature. Microwave vegetables in covered glass dish for 3 minutes. Cool to room temperature; turn into salad bowl. Break fish into bite-size pieces. Add fish and shrimp to vegetables. Pour dressing over top. Toss gently. Chill thoroughly before serving.

To prepare vinaigrette dressing, combine all ingredients in a jar. Shake well to blend.

Leo G. J. Seffelaar
Broadview, Saskatchewan, Canada

Fish:

1 lb. snapper or cod

2 cups coarsely chopped green beans

1 cup sliced carrots

1 cup shrimp

Vinaigrette:

1 tsp. salt

$1/2$ tsp. dry mustard

$1/4$ tsp. pepper

$1/2$ cup olive oil

2 T. red wine vingar

2 T. finely chopped onion

1 tsp. tarragon

1 tsp. sugar

137

Bonito Casserole

Bake bonito at 350 degrees for 15 minutes or until flaky. Chop bonito; set aside. Cook broccoli according to package directions; drain. In large saucepan, heat olive oil. Blend in salt, flour and milk. Stir until thickened and bubbly. Add Parmesan cheese, lemon juice and dillweed. Stir in broccoli, mushrooms and chopped bonito. Pour into 2 quart casserole dish. Bake at 350 degrees for 30 minutes. Cut refrigerated biscuits into quarters. Arrange quarters around edge of hot casserole dish; bake 15 minutes longer.

Jack D. Hunter
Harlingen, TX

1 lb. bonito fillet

2 (10-oz.) pkg. frozen broccoli

6 T. olive oil

1 tsp. salt

$1/2$ cup flour

$3^1/2$ cups milk

$1/3$ cup grated Parmesan cheese

1 T. lemon juice

$1/2$ tsp. dried dillweed

1 small jar mushrooms

1 pkg. refrigerated biscuits

138

Bonito Casserole

Halibut and Fruit Broil

2 halibut steaks

2 T. butter, melted

2 T. lemon juice

Salt

Pepper

Paprika

1 large orange, peeled, sliced

*1 banana, peeled, halved lengthwise,
cut into thirds*

Barbecue Sea Bass

4 sea bass fillets

1 bottle barbecue sauce

Seasoned salt

1 Bermuda onion, chopped

Place halibut on well-oiled broiler pan. Brush with melted butter, reserving some for later use. Season lemon juice with salt, pepper and paprika. Sprinkle with half the seasoned lemon juice. Broil 4 inches from heat source for 5 minutes or until lightly browned. Arrange fruit sections around halibut. Brush fruit and fish with remaining melted butter. Season again with lemon juice, salt, pepper and paprika. Broil another 5 minutes or until halibut juices run clear and flesh is opaque when fork-tested.

Leo G. J. Seffelaar
Broadview, Saskatchewan, Canada

Roll fillets in barbecue sauce. Place on aluminum foil; sprinkle with seasoned salt. Add onions to top of fillet. Wrap in foil; lay on grill for 5-6 minutes on each side.

Robert Greggs
Augusta, WV

Navy Black and Blues

Place fillets in large shallow glass baking dish. Add water to cover fish. Add lemon slices and ice. Soak for 1½ hours. Dry fillets with paper towels. Place fillets into egg whites. Roll fillets in crushed chips; coating both sides. Lightly spray foil with nonstick cooking spray. Place fillets on foil. Bake at 375 degrees for 20-25 minutes. After baking, briefly broil fish to crisp top of fish. Prepare rice. In saucepan, heat olive oil. Add garlic; brown. Add beans; simmer for 5 minutes. Add onions to beans; turn burner off. On serving platter, prepare bed of cooked rice, beans and fillets. Garnish platter with pimentos, green olives and limes. Top with fresh cilantro. Serve salsa on the side.

Richard Zablauskas
Bronx, NY

4-6 bluefish fillets

Bottled spring water

2 lemons, thinly sliced

Ice

3-4 egg whites, beaten

1 bag blue corn chips, crushed

1 pkg. yellow rice

3 tsp. olive oil

2 cloves garlic, minced

16-oz. can black beans, crushed

1 medium yellow onion, diced

Pimentos

Spanish green olives

2 fresh limes, quartered

Fresh cilantro

Salsa

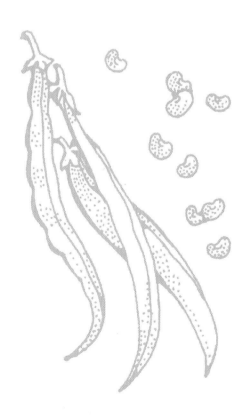

Country Garden Sauté

Country Garden Sauté

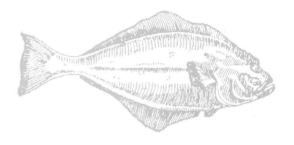

Remove bones and skin from fish. Cut into 1-inch cubes. Season with pepper; set aside. In large skillet, heat oil over medium-high heat. Add vegetables and water. Sauté until tender crisp. Add fish to skillet. Combine broth, cornstarch, ginger and lemon peel. Add to fish and vegetables. Cook and stir until thickened and fish flakes easily when fork-tested. Serve with steamed rice.

Leslie J. Richardson
San Benito, TX

1 lb. halibut or cod

Pepper

1 T. olive oil

1 cup sliced carrots

1 cup diagonally sliced green onions

1 cup broccoli florets

1 cup sliced fresh mushrooms

$\frac{1}{4}$ cup water

$\frac{1}{4}$ cup chicken broth

2 tsp. cornstarch

$\frac{1}{4}$ tsp. grated fresh ginger

1 tsp. grated lemon peel

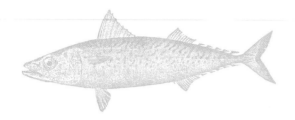

Bacon Wrapped Mackerel

Fish:

3 mackerel steaks

12 bacon strips

Sauce:

1 bunch parsley, chopped

2 cloves garlic, chopped

2 T. Worcestershire sauce

$^{1}/_{4}$ cup olive oil

$^{1}/_{2}$ tsp. salt

Cut mackerel into medallions. Wrap with bacon slice; secure with toothpick. Grill until fish is cooked and bacon is crispy. Combine all sauce ingredients together; top fish. Note: sauce is best if made 1-2 days before.

James Didier II
New Orleans, LA

Pacific Fish Florentine

$1^{1}/_{2}$ lbs. Pacific fish steaks or fillets

Flour

4 T. Butter

Salt

Pepper

2 cups chopped fresh spinach, cooked

$^{1}/_{4}$ tsp. nutmeg

1 clove garlic, crushed

2 T. lemon juice

$^{1}/_{2}$ tsp. crushed fennel seeds

Dust fish with flour. Heat 2 tablespoons butter in skillet. Sauté fish for 10 minutes per inch thickness. Turn once halfway through cooking period. Season with salt and pepper. Season hot spinach with nutmeg; place on heated platter. Arrange fish portion on spinach; keep warm. Add remaining butter and garlic to skillet. Cook, stirring until butter starts to color; discard garlic. Stir in lemon juice and fennel; pour over fish.

Leo G. J. Seffelaar
Broadview, Saskatchewan, Canada

Healthy Halibut

4 (4-oz.) fresh halibut steaks

$^1/_3$ cup finely minced onions

1 clove garlic, minced

2 T. minced fresh parsley

$^1/_2$ tsp. finely shredded orange peel

$^1/_8$ tsp. black pepper

$^1/_4$ cup fresh orange juice

1 T. fresh lemon juice

Arrange fish steaks in 8 x 8 x 2-inch baking dish; set aside. Lightly spray skillet with nonstick cooking spray. Add onions and garlic. Cook and stir over medium heat until onions are tender. Remove skillet from heat. Stir in parsley, orange peel and pepper. Spread onion mixture over fish. Mix orange and lemon juice. Pour juice mixture over fish. Cover with foil. Bake halibut steaks at 400 degrees for 12-15 minutes or until fish flakes easily. Serve with rice and button mushrooms.

Paul Wells
Sierra Vista, AZ

Salt Baked Grouper

1 grouper, gutted

3 sprigs thyme

2 sprigs basil

1 head garlic

1 lemon

3 lbs. kosher salt

Place grouper in baking pan. Combine herbs, garlic and lemon. Stuff cavity with mixture. Cover entirely with kosher salt. Bake for 1$^1/_2$ hours. Crack open salt dome; brush off fish. Peel back skin; spoon flesh off.

James Didier II
New Orleans, LA

Halibut Potato Bake

1½ lbs. potatoes, peeled, thinly sliced

6 T. olive oil

1 T. minced garlic

⅓ cup chopped parsley

Salt

Pepper

1½ lbs. halibut steaks or fillets

Halibut Gumbo

1 gallon chicken stock

Chili powder

Gumbo file

Sassafras leaves

Tabasco sauce

2 cups rice

2 cups okra

2 cups chopped onion

2-4 cups cubed halibut

Place potatoes in bowl of cold water. Drain; pat dry. In measuring cup combine oil, garlic and parsley. In 9 x 10-inch baking dish, mix potatoes with half seasoned oil. Sprinkle with salt and pepper. Bake at 450 degrees for 15 minutes or until potatoes are nearly tender. Remove from oven; place halibut on potatoes. Drizzle with remaining oil; sprinkle with salt and pepper. Bake 10-15 minutes, basting occasionally with pan juices. Halibut is done when juices run clear and flesh is opaque.

Leo G. J. Seffelaar
Broadview, Saskatchewan, Canada

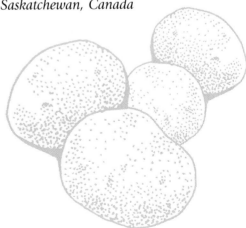

Boil chicken stock. Add chili powder, gumbo file, sassafras leaves and Tabasco to taste. Add 2 cups rice, simmer for 1 hour. Add okra, onion and halibut. Cook for 10 minutes.

Clint Hooper
Camarillo, CA

Snapper Stew

1 small onion, chopped

1 small zucchini, sliced

1 stalk celery, chopped

3 T. olive oil

4 medium ripe tomatoes,
peeled, chopped

$\frac{1}{2}$ cup fish or chicken stock

1 tsp. sugar

$\frac{1}{2}$ tsp. rosemary

1 clove garlic, crushed

3 T. flour

3 T. water

1 lb. snapper fillets,
cut into 1-inch cubes

Cook onion, zucchini, celery and olive oil in large saucepan over medium heat. Vegetables should be tender crisp. Add tomatoes, stock, sugar, rosemary and garlic. Cover; simmer for 10 minutes. Mix flour and water; add to saucepan. Cook, stirring constantly until sauce bubbles and thickens. Add snapper; cook over low heat until flesh is opaque and begins to open into flakes. Serve immediately with rice, pasta or potatoes.

Leo G. J. Seffelaar
Broadview, Saskatchewan, Canada

Last Minute Mackerel

1 stick butter

3-5 lbs. king mackerel

$\frac{1}{2}$ onion, diced

1 green pepper, diced

Place butter in saucepan. Melt over medium heat. When almost completely melted, add mackerel, onion and green pepper. Turn heat very low; cover. Cook 1-1$\frac{1}{2}$ hours or until fish is white and flaky. Stir occasionally; making sure fish is broken up. Serve in bowl with oyster crackers on the side.

A. Allen
Via e-mail

ACCOMPANIMENTS

Fish is great, but in most cases

a fish meal just isn't complete without

a special accompaniment, side dish or sauce

to round everything out. In many cases,

these fish-cooking traditions are

as important as the fish itself!

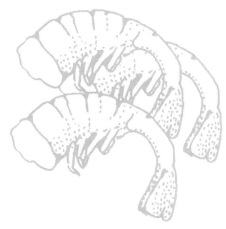

Spicy Seafood Sauce

1/2 cup ketchup

1 T. coarse ground horseradish

1/8 tsp. ground cayenne pepper

Dash of lemon pepper

Combine all ingredients; mix well. Keep chilled.

Cam Powers
Mason City, IA

Vinaigrette Dressing

1 tsp. salt

1/2 tsp. dry mustard

1/4 tsp. pepper

1/2 cup olive oil

2 T. red wine vinegar

2 tsp. finely chopped onion

1 tsp. tarragon

1 tsp. sugar

Combine all ingredients in jar with lid. Shake well to blend. This can be used as fish marinade as well as salad dressing.

Leo Seffelaar
Broadview, Saskatchewan, Canada

Marinade for Fish

1/8 cup soy sauce

1/2 cup water

1 onion, chopped

1 clove garlic

1/8 cup sesame oil

Combine all ingredients. Soak fish fillets and refrigerate overnight. Grill, bake, broil or fry fish.

Herb Terry
Chickasha, OK

Fresh Horseradish Sauce

1 cup chopped horseradish root

¾ cup white vinegar

1-2 T. sugar

¼ tsp. salt

Finely grate all ingredients in blender until well mixed.

James and Cindy Bell
Ft. Lewis, WA

Tom's Fish Dip Mix

1 cup crushed crackers

2 cups flour

2 T. lemon pepper

1 T. minced dried onion

1 T. seasoned salt

1 T. garlic salt

1 T. black pepper

2 eggs, beaten

Garlic Walleye Cheeks

24 medium walleye cheeks, skinned

Water

Salt

¼ lb. Italian garlic spread

Place cheeks in medium saucepan. Cover with water. Salt lightly; boil. In separate pan, melt garlic spread. When cheeks are tender, drain. Place cheeks in small bowl; pour melted garlic spread over cheeks. Serve as an appetizer.

D. Kulas
Cleveland, OH

Combine all ingredients except eggs. Dip fish of choice into beaten eggs. Roll fish in dry mix and fry in oil.

Tom Sager
Seymour, IA

Hush Puppies

1 bottle vegetable oil

1 cup yellow cornmeal

$^1/_3$ cup flour

1 tsp. sugar

1 tsp. baking powder

Salt

$^1/_8$ tsp. cayenne pepper

1 egg

$^1/_4$ cup chopped onion

8-oz. can cream-style corn

2 T. buttermilk

Heat oil in deep fryer. Mix cornmeal, flour, sugar, baking powder, salt and cayenne. Stir in remaining ingredients until combined. Drop batter by tablespoonful into hot oil. Cook until golden brown, about 4-5 minutes. Drain on paper towels.

Roland J. Cote III
Waterville, ME

Tartar Sauce

$^1/_2$ cup mayonnaise

2 dill pickles

1 tsp. lemon juice

1 slice onion

3 sprigs parsley

Mix all ingredients in blender or food processor until well blended.

James and Cindy Bell
Ft. Lewis, WA

Fish Spread or Dip

2 cups fish, broiled

8-oz. pkg. cream cheese

$^1/_4$ cup lemon juice

$^1/_8$ T. Tabasco sauce

1 small onion, grated

$^1/_2$ cup mayonnaise

Place all ingredients in blender. Mix well. Use as a spread for crackers or as a dip for chips.

Herb Terry
Chickasha, OK

Fish Spread
or Dip

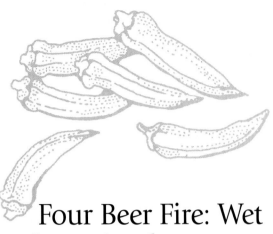

Four Beer Fire: Wet Jerk Marinade (Very Hot!)

Mix all ingredients to make thick paste. Add water as necessary. Place mixture in blender to combine. Slather sauce on fish fillets; grill over medium-hot fire. Serve with corn-on-the-cob.

Mr. Rob Wodzinski
Iron River, MI

10 Scotch bonnet or habanero chiles

6 cloves garlic

2 T. fresh ginger

1 tsp. grated nutmeg

$1/4$ tsp. cinnamon

2 T. allspice

$1/4$ tsp. ground cloves

2 T. dillweed

2 T. black peppercorns

3 T. salt

1 bunch chives, chopped

1 bunch scallions, chopped

1 large onion, chopped

$1/4$ cup oil

3 T. brown sugar

$1/4$ lime juice

$1/4$ cup white vinegar

$1/4$ cup water

$1/2$ cup dark rum

Hush Puppies

1³/4 cups cornbread mix

¹/3 cup milk

2 eggs

¹/3 cup finely chopped onion

Thoroughly combine all ingredients. Drop by teaspoonful into hot oil; fry until golden brown.

William Baker
Deltona, FL

Chilled Jalapeño Hollandaise

4 jalapeños, seeded

3 egg yolks

Juice of 2 limes

2 tsp. grated garlic

1¹/2 tsp. salt

²/3 cup rice vinegar

4 cups vegetable oil

2 oz. water

Place all ingredients except water and oil in food processor. Puree on high for 2 minutes. Turn speed down to medium; slowly add in oil then water. Refrigerate until needed. Great topping for shore lunch fish fry.

Karl Ulmer
Hawley, PA

155